Family Walks
in
East Sussex

Sally and Clive Cutter

HIGH INTEREST · LOW MILEAGE

Scarthin Books of Cromford
Derbyshire
1994

Family Walks Series

The Country Code

Guard against all risk of fire
Fasten all gates
Keep your dogs under proper control
Keep to public paths across farmland
Avoid damaging fences, hedges and walls
Leave no litter
Safeguard water supplies
Make no unnecessary noise
Protect wildlife, plants and trees
Go carefully along country roads
Respect the life of the countryside

Published 1994

Phototypesetting by Paragon Typesetters, Queensferry, Clwyd

Printed by Redwood Books

ISBN 0 907758 71 1

Cover illustration by Ron Muschamp. *Seven Sisters Cliff (route 8)*

Stile in Buxted Deer Park, looking into Manor Park (route 4)

Dedication

To Sally's mum, Joan.

Acknowledgements

Thanks to Dorothy for her company on many of the walks and also to Pat for her good-humoured support.

About the authors

Sally was born in Dulwich and has lived mainly in Orpington. Clive was born in Zimbabwe and came to England in 1978. They now live in Orpington, which has proved an ideal base for their countryside explorations of Kent and Sussex.

Contents

Map of the area

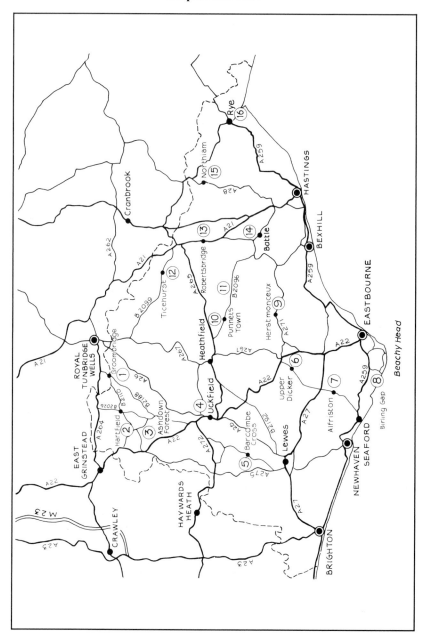

Introduction

Constant variety is the essence of the beauty of East Sussex, adding both to its richness and at the same time making it a fascinating prospect for exploration. From the ancient sandstone outcrops of Harrison's Rocks in the northern part of the county, which were formed about a hundred million years ago, to the lovely Ashdown Forest and the gently rolling hills around Hartfield in the west, which is of course Pooh Bear country, and from the long white line of the Seven Sisters Cliff beside Birling Gap on the south coast, which used to be a landing point for smugglers, to the flat stark isolation of the Rye Harbour Nature Reserve in the east, where visitors can watch from two specially built hides which are open to the public, there is something for everyone.

Family walks

Potential newcomers to the increasingly popular activity of countryside walking might hardly be blamed for wondering what all the fuss is about. After all it can get rather muddy in the fields after rain and in dry weather sections of the ground can become inconveniently hard and uneven. So why do people do it? The reason is simple and is out there just waiting to be found. It can be heard in the birdsong, in the chiming of village church bells and in the tinkling of water over stones in a stream, it can be seen in the shimmering blue of distant hills, in the petals of a wildflower and in the eyes of a little lamb, it can be felt in the breeze, in the natural glow of exercise and in the openness, a release from the closely pressing strains of routine daily life.

For children, and perhaps too for many of their parents, the often-dreaded subject of history might suddenly take on a new depth of meaning as they stand at the edge of the largest moat in England, actually part of the River Cuckmere, which circles the magnificent Michelham Priory near Upper Dicker, or perhaps as they gaze in awe across the fields at Herstmonceux Castle, which reputedly has a chimney for every Sunday and a window for every day of the year, or of course when they visit the famous town of Battle and tread in the footsteps of the Saxon and Norman soldiers who clashed so violently in the Battle of Hastings in 1066.

No chance now, though, as the family strolls through a largely heathland section of the Ashdown Forest, of seeing the giant lizards that used to roam the area in Prehistoric times, although the thought itself is quite dramatic! The history of the Sussex smugglers too is sure to capture many a lively imagination on a walk around Alfriston, home of the infamous Alfriston Gang. The Old Clergy House can also be visited in this beautiful village. It was bought for £10 in 1896 by the National Trust, their first acquisition. And for other outings there's the wonderful Buxted Deer Park near Uckfield or the charming countryside around Punnett's Town, where the gleaming white Blackdown Mill sits on the top of a hill as if at the top of the world; or Bewl Water near Ticehurst or perhaps Robertsbridge, set in the valley of the River Rother, the surrounding area so laced with streams that there is an abundance of delightful bridges.

Symbols used on the route maps

- - ► - - ► - - ►	Route (right of way unless otherwise stated)
....	Footpath (not on route)
= = = = = = = = =	Track
════════════	Road
┼┼┼┼┼┼┼┼┼┼┼	Railway
～～～～～	River/stream
Village	Village

Woodland	Woodland
Cliffs/Rocks	Cliffs/Rocks
Lake	Lake
■	Building(s)
+	Church
	Car Park
	Pond
	Number corresponds with route description

Harrison's Rocks

Outline

Ayttons Wood car park — Harrison's Rocks — Birchden Forge and Forge Farm — Pinstraw Farm — Ayttons Wood car park.

Summary

The gap in ages between children and their parents may appear to shrink dramatically in relative terms as the family shares a sense of wonder at the thought that the famous Harrison's Rocks are over a hundred million years old. One of many sandstone outcrops in the region (other notable examples being High Rocks and Wellington Rocks in neighbouring Kent), they are part of the Hastings Sand belt and were formed as a result of gradual sedimentation on the floor of the great Wealden Lake which used to cover the whole of south east England and part of the Continent. Today, standing in places up to forty feet high, the lengthy face of the rocks, smoothed and shaped by centuries of frost and rain, makes an impressive sight. So too does the surrounding farmland, a chance for children once again to share with their parents in an appreciation of the environment, not only the far-reaching views in all directions, but also the many animals along the way, such as horses, cattle and sheep, not forgetting in spring the always appealing sight of frisky little lambs in the fields.

Attractions

Getting to grips with the nature of the rocks in a more physical sense, climbers have been visiting the area since the middle of the 19th century. Offering a wide range of shapes, heights and degrees of difficulty, Harrison's Rocks have become known as an ideal practice ground for the sport, both for beginners and more advanced enthusiasts. The dangers of course are obvious and any newcomers wishing to join in should make enquiries first with local climbing associations, schools or boys' and girls' activity clubs. Having said that, the sight of determined adventurers grappling with challenging hand-holds and balancing on narrow ledges might perhaps provide as much entertainment for spectators as the actual brave participants themselves.

In the early part of the walk there are plenty of safe wide open spaces for children to romp about, while older members of the party might look out for a rich display of birds and wildflowers. Tiny wrens, red-breasted robins and the distinctive black-capped and yellow-sided great tits, with their high-pitched call very similar to a squeaky gate, may all add enjoyment to the outing and in spring white wood anemones, yellow lesser celandine, lemon-petalled primroses and, a little later, bluebells provide lovely splashes of colour beside the footpaths.

Once through the beautiful grounds of Birchden Forge and past the double oasts of Forge Farm, which is backed by a picturesque gently meandering stream, the route passes between two long lines of mixed hedgerows, including hawthorn with its

Continued on page 12

9

Route 1

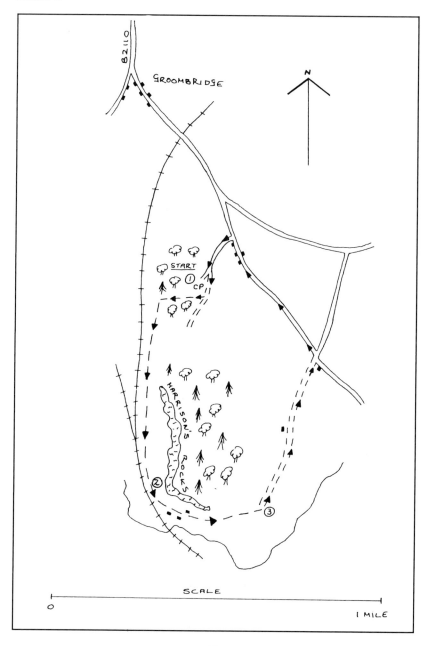

Route 1

Harrison's Rocks   2½ miles

Start

At Ayttons Wood car park at the end of a signposted lane to Harrison's Rocks (OS Pathfinder 1248 GR 534365), off the road to Eridge Station about half a mile south of Groombridge. Approached by either the B2110 or the A26.

Route

1. *Leave car park through main entrance. Turn right into a track. After about 50 yards/metres turn right downhill along gravel footpath indicated by yellow arrow (High Weald Walk). After about 200 yards/metres cross over a stile and continue along indicated path through a field. Turn left and follow indicated path running parallel with a railway line. Continue straight ahead beside railway line as Harrison's Rocks come into view on the left. Pass through a gap in a hedge and continue along indicated path beside railway line.*

2. *Cross a stile into grounds of Birchden Forge and continue straight ahead along indicated footpath. Pass through gateway and proceed along track beside farm buildings. Continue straight ahead through another gateway and then after about a further 100 yards/metres cross a stile. Continue uphill along indicated footpath. Cross over another stile and continue straight ahead along path.*

3. *At the top of the hill bear left along path as it leads into a grassy track. Proceed along track, eventually crossing a stile beside a gate and then continuing straight ahead along a tarmac track. On eventually reaching a lane turn left in direction of sign to Groombridge (CAUTION). Continue along lane for about half a mile and then turn left into indicated lane to Harrison's Rocks. Follow lane to car park.*

Access by bus
To Groombridge from Tunbridge Wells.

Alder: cones (female) and catkins (male)

11

delicately maturing blossom in early summer and its bright red berries in autumn and also honeysuckle, charging the air on a hot summer's day with its sweet, heady fragrance.

The short stretch along the lane towards Groombridge near the end of the walk is usually fairly quiet, although some care should be taken of youngsters in case of speeding cars. More lovely views of the surrounding rolling hills can be enjoyed along this section of the route.

Refreshments
A snack stall in Ayttons Wood car park or a picnic along the route. Or perhaps The Junction public house in nearby Groombridge.

Climbing at Harrison's Rocks

Hartfield

Outline
Hartfield – Hewkins Bridge – Top Hill Farm – Ash Corner Wood – Hartfield.

Summary
This is the stomping ground of Christopher Robin and Pooh Bear, who will need no introduction to children and the young-at-heart of all ages throughout the world. The amusing and often deeply touching stories of their adventures are doubtless amongst the favourites of many enthusiastic fans. With a challenging inventory of stiles, footbridges, hills to climb and fields to cross, as well as a host of real-life friendly animal faces along the way, this route should not only provide the family with a wonderful opportunity to enjoy their own adventure in this delightful pocket of the East Sussex countryside, but might also infuse some visitors with a hint of that inspirational magic that led to the creation of Winnie-the-Pooh by A.A. Milne at his home on Cotchford Farm, just south of Hartfield.

Attractions
Situated on a slope above the River Medway, Hartfield was originally little more than a clearing made in the vast Wealden Forest for the grazing of deer, to which it owes its name. Starting at the 13th century church of St Mary the Virgin, the route passes through a wide open area known as Fourteen Acre Pit, offering a lovely view of Forstal Farm to the right and the rolling hills behind it. Soon afterwards a second panoramic view is unveiled, with the pretty ponds and meandering stream beside Hewkins Bridge, where geese might be seen basking on the grassy banks. Beyond, on the side of another hill, the tower of the 17th century church at Withyham.

Joining a section of the Wealdway the route then passes through more farmland before running for a short distance along the bank of the River Medway, where willows flourish and, in spring, splashes of bluebells light up the greenery beneath the trees. A fairly long climb leads to Top Hill Farm and the Wanstead Stud, with horses grazing contentedly in its picturesque wooden-fenced paddocks and on occasion a spindly-legged foal innocently tottering at their sides. The views from the approach to the farm, looking back over the valley, are spectacular: to the left, fronted by the triple oasts of Summerford Farm, is the small settlement of Ball's Green, while over to the right is Withyham, the tower of its church visible above the trees.

Heading back towards Hartfield the route then passes through the small yet beautiful Ash Corner Wood, a haven for wildflowers. Between the months of April and June the air is rich with the smell of garlic, emanating from a plant by the name of ramsons, part of the lily family, their longish pale green pods opening to reveal little white flowers. Reputedly appearing when the cuckoo arrives, the lovely lilac-coloured cuckoo flower or lady's smock can also be seen here, along with the star-shaped, white-petalled greater stitchwort, as well as violets and primroses.

Route 2

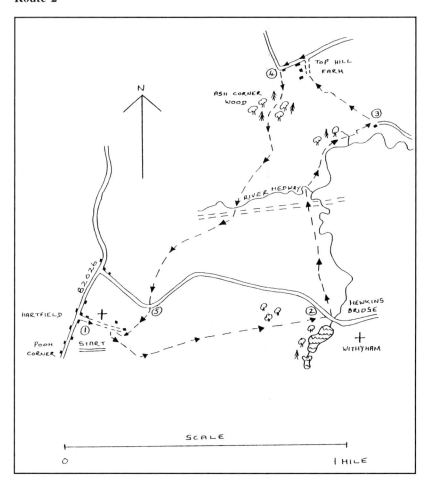

TOP HILL FARM

④

③

ASH CORNER WOOD

N

RIVER MEDWAY

HEWKINS BRIDGE

B2026

HARTFIELD

⑤

②

POOH CORNER

① START

WITHYHAM

SCALE

0   1 MILE

Route 2

Hartfield   4 miles

Start

In Church Street (beside the Anchor Inn) off High Street (OS Pathfinder 1248 GR 479357), which is part of the B2026. Limited parking in Church Street or in the village.

Route

1. Walk to end of Church Street and continue straight ahead as it leads into a track. After about 50 yards/metres turn right and cross a stile. Turn left and proceed along border of a field. Cross over another stile beside a gate and proceed along left border of another field. Cross over a stile, turn left and after 5 yards/metres cross over another stile on the right. Proceed diagonally towards the left through another field. Cross over a stile beside a gateway and proceed diagonally towards the right through yet another field, continuing over the brow of a hill and eventually crossing a stile in the far right-hand corner to reach a lane.

2. Turn right along lane (CAUTION). After about 20 yards/metres (just before Hewkins Bridge) cross over a stile on the left. Bearing slightly left cross through a field (Wealdway). Cross over a stile and, bearing slightly right, cross through another field. Cross over a stile, then a track and then another stile. Continue straight ahead through a field and then cross over a footbridge. Proceed straight ahead through another field. Continue along indicated path leading first beside the river (CAUTION) and then up a short slope. Turn right along indicated path. Continue as path runs alongside a fence. Cross over a small footbridge and continue uphill along path. Cross over a stile on the left and then turn right along indicated path.

3. After about 100 yards/metres (just before reaching a gateway) turn sharp left and proceed uphill diagonally through field in direction of yellow arrow. Cross over a stile in top left corner and follow indicated path along right border of another field. After only 20 yards/metres turn right and cross over another stile. Follow indicated path between wooden fences. Cross over another stile and walk along right border of farmyard to reach a lane. Turn left and proceed along lane in direction of yellow arrow.

4. Pass through a gateway at right-hand bend in lane and turn left. Proceed in direction of sign along footpath leading between a barn on the left and a field on the right. Continue along path as it leads between a hedge and a fence and then through a wood. On leaving wood follow path along left border of a field. After about 150 yards/metres turn right along indicated path leading downhill through

Continued on page 16

15

the field. Continue downhill in direction of footpath sign and then cross over a footbridge. Cross over a stile, then a track and then another stile. Follow indicated path diagonally towards the right through a field. Leave field through a gate in far right corner and follow indicated path along right border of another field. Pass through another gateway and proceed along right border of another field. On reaching two adjacent stiles cross over left stile and follow indicated path through a field, eventually crossing another stile into a lane (CAUTION).

5. *Cross over lane and then a stile beside a gate. Follow indicated path along right border of a field, eventually crossing over a stile in far right corner. Turn right and follow pathway back to Church Street.*

Access by bus
To Hartfield from Tunbridge Wells and East Grinstead.

Refreshments
The Anchor Inn or Hay Waggon Inn, tea at Stairs Farm House or perhaps an ice cream from Pooh Corner. Or, of course, a picnic on the route.

Pooh Corner

Duddleswell (Ashdown Forest)

Outline
Duddleswell − Marlpits − Duddleswell.

Summary
The Ashdown Forest is all that remains of a vast forest that once covered most of Sussex. This route passes through a small section of it, mostly open heathland, dotted on the fringes with oaks and silver birch. The starting point is at Duddleswell (Duddell's spring), a former Royal Manor, which in the 14th century was one of six royal walks in the old Deer Forest or Royal Forest (Silva Regalis). Offering a seemingly endless catalogue of panoramic views, at first towards the south over the lovely line of the South Downs, the route soon swings round, heading northwards towards an area known as Marlpits, which at the time of the restoration of Charles II (1660) was a new enclosure in the forest Sweet Minepits, a leftover of the iron industry. Further magnificent views towards the south can be enjoyed as the route then follows a long, wide, grassy pathway along the side of a hill before swinging once again towards Duddleswell.

Attractions
Children and parents alike may find it fascinating to consider that in Prehistoric times huge lizards roamed about in the area together with wolves and wild boar. It was the early Celtic settlers in the initial days of the Iron Age who first began to clear the Great Wealden Forest which at that time started in East Kent and ran between the North and South Downs all the way to Hampshire. Next came the Romans in AD43, developing the iron industry and building their villas, bathhouses and a highway through the Ashdown Forest, which they knew as Sylva Anderida. Then it was the turn of the Saxons who called the forest Andreaswald, although just like their successors, the Normans, they remained mainly on its outer fringes.

It was really only during the Middle Ages and the days of The Cinque Ports that the great assault on the forest began in earnest. The iron industry was revived and oaks were extensively felled for shipbuilding, especially during The Hundred Years War with France. Concern about the staggering depletion of trees reached a head in 1607 and a halt was finally called to the destruction.

Today, in the area around Duddleswell, it is heather, gorse, bracken and horses, together with a wonderful atmosphere of peace that the modern visitor can expect to find, with plenty of ideal picnic spots and safe areas where children can run about. Being so open and so hilly it can also be very windy − good for blowing away the cobwebs though, and perfect for youngsters, whether experts or newcomers, to have a go at flying a kite. And on the subject of aeronautics, a natural flier in the neighbourhood to look out for is the beautiful yellowhammer, a typical heathland bird with a striking mustard-coloured breast.   *Continued on page 20*

Route 3

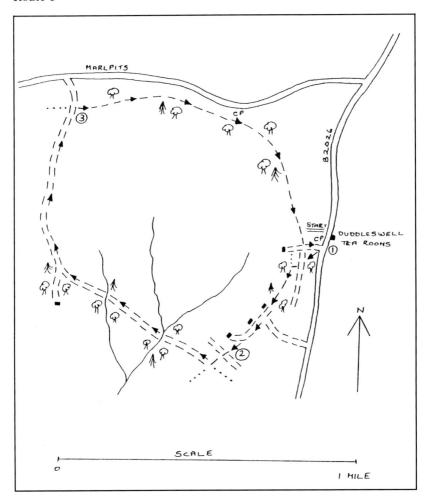

Route 3

Duddleswell (Ashdown Forest)   3½ miles

Start

At the Duddleswell car park (OS Pathfinder 1269 GR 468279), on the B2026 (about 6 miles south of Hartfield).

Route

1. *Turn right from the entrance of Duddleswell car park into B2026 (CAUTION). After about 20 yards/metres turn right into indicated public footpath. On reaching a dirt track turn left. After about a further 20 yards/metres turn right into a footpath. On reaching an intersection of paths turn left. Continue along path which eventually leads into a driveway beside Little Gassons. Proceed along driveway for a further 20 yards/metres, then bear right into a dirt track, continuing as this track leads into another tarmac driveway. Continue along driveway past Larkrise on the right. After about a further 100 yards/metres (as driveway swings to the right) bear left along a wide grassy footpath.*

2. *Continue straight across a track and after a further 10 yards/metres turn right at a second track. Continue along track down a very steep slope, crossing a stream at the bottom via stepping stones. Continue straight ahead up a steep dirt track. Cross over the brow of the hill and then proceed downhill along same track. Cross over another stream via more stepping stones and then continue uphill along track. On reaching an intersection with a gravel driveway turn right. Proceed uphill along driveway.*

3. *At the top of the hill (just before driveway swings to the left to meet a road) turn right, passing beside a log barrier and then proceed along a wide grassy pathway. Continue along path as it bears slightly left and then continue straight ahead as it runs for some distance parallel to the road. On reaching a small car park continue straight ahead along path up a hill. Continue over brow of hill and follow clearly visible wide, winding pathway, eventually turning left into a tarmac driveway to reach Duddleswell car park.*

Access by bus
To Duddleswell from Uckfield and Tunbridge Wells.

Finally, the story of the nearby Nutley Mill shouldn't be left out of the picture either. Both the oldest and the smallest working windmill in Sussex, it was actually built in 1675 at Crowborough or possibly Goudhurst and was moved to Nutley in 1810. An open-trestle post mill, without a roundhouse or fantail, it ceased commercial work in 1908 and was restored to working order in 1971 by the Uckfield and District Preservation Society.

Refreshments
At the Duddleswell Tea Rooms or a picnic along the way.

Path through Ashdown Forest

Uckfield and Buxted Deer Park

Outline
Uckfield — Manor Park — Buxted Deer Park — Uckfield.

Summary
From the school playing fields near Uckfield High Street a lovely view over the valley of the River Uck and the hills behind it seems to beckon the explorer. A relaxing shady footpath follows before the route joins a section of the Wealdway beside the beautiful Hempstead Mill, leading for a short distance along the bank of the river. Moving on into Buxted Deer Park and then briefly dipping into a corner of Manor Park, a haven of cooling shade in hot weather, the path crosses through the lawns in front of the Buxted Park Hotel and then through the churchyard of Buxted Parish Church. The return through the lower part of the deer park passes two very pretty ponds, one on either side of the path, before once again linking with the earlier part of the walk along the peaceful tree-lined riverside.

Attractions
The lovely houses and gardens in Hempstead Lane and the heavenly setting of Hempstead Mill, with its strikingly high black spiral staircase, set the scene for a walk full of charm and beauty. The almost blue and silver sheen of willow leaves and the darker foliage of the alders which overhang the lazily meandering River Uck provide a wonderful atmosphere, a place where fishermen while away the hours and where, through the trees on the other side of the river, cattle and horses might be seen grazing in lush green pastures.

The expanse and openness of Buxted Deer Park, where deer might be spotted amongst the carpets of bracken which grow tall in the summer, makes an interesting contrast before a brief visit into the woods of Manor Park, the only disturbance of the peace as such being the call of the birds in the trees or the tinkling of a little stream at the bottom of a hill. Turning away just before the stream the route re-enters the deer park before passing in front of the exclusive Buxted Park Hotel, the building dating back to 1726, its lawns dotted with oaks, sweet chestnuts, horse chestnuts and limes. The chiming of Buxted Parish Church bells is attractively unusual and from the gate at the back of the churchyard a sweeping view awaits of the valley below and the village of Buxted on the side of the hill beyond.

The final stretch of the walk along another wide grassy pathway, which in places is lined with tall lime trees, leads past two large ponds, an ideal place for a picnic, where swans, ducks and geese might be seen as well as electric blue damsel flies and where fish might be spotted gliding in the cool depths of the water or occasionally, with a slapping, popping sound, rising suddenly and breaking through the surface. A second pleasant stroll along the bank of the River Uck leads back to Uckfield, where, especially on a hot summer's day and especially for the children, a swim at Utopia, Uckfield's Leisure Centre, might prove the perfect end to a perfect outing.

Route 4

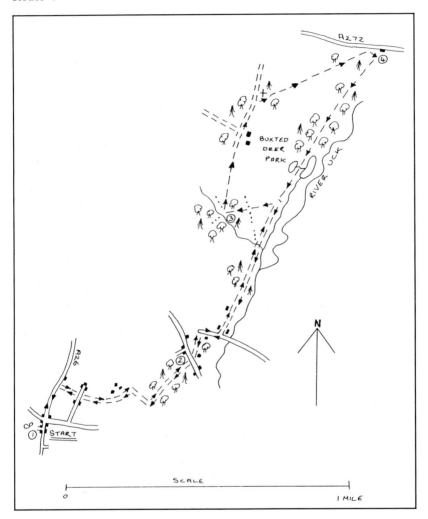

Route 4

Uckfield and Buxted Deer Park   4½ miles

Start

At the public car park in the High Street (A26) next to the library (entrance between The Picture House and Town Hall) (OS Pathfinder 1269 GR 473213).

Route

1. *Turn left into High Street from car park entrance. Proceed up High Street past Ye Maidens Head and The Chalk and Cheese. Turn right into Bedford Court (indicated by stone footpath sign). Continue straight ahead as Bedford Court leads into footpath. Cross over a road and continue along footpath. Continue straight ahead through car park (Utopia Leisure Centre) and turn left along edge of playing field. Turn right at end of playing field and proceed downhill along footpath. Pass through a gateway and down a small flight of steps. Turn left into a tarmac footpath, continuing to reach a road.*

2. *Cross over road (CAUTION) and follow tarmac footpath directly opposite. Continue along path, which leads into Hempstead Lane, following it downhill as it swings to the right. Just before reaching the river turn left into a gravel road indicated by yellow arrow as Wealdway. Proceed along road past Hempstead Mill, continuing straight ahead as road leads into a footpath. Follow footpath along bank of river. Cross over a footbridge and continue along path, keeping to the right at a fork. Cross over a stile and then turn left, following indicated footpath. Cross over a stile beside a gate and continue along indicated Wealdway. At an intersection of paths continue straight ahead along path leading into woods. Cross over a stile and continue downhill through woods.*

3. *Just before a bridge turn right along indicated Wealdway. On reaching a fork take path leading uphill to the right. Cross over a stile and continue straight ahead through a field. Cross over a stile beside a gate into Buxted Park and cross through a field in direction of yellow arrow. Continue as path leads into driveway, proceeding past front of Buxted Park Hotel (in direction of footpath sign). Continue straight ahead along driveway towards church. Turn right along indicated footpath leading through churchyard, leaving through a gate at the back. Bearing slightly towards the left follow wide grassy footpath downhill through field.*

4. *Just before reaching a gate at the bottom of the hill bear right along smaller path and then after only 20 yards/metres turn sharp right along another wide grassy pathway. Continue along path, eventually passing a pond on the left and then one on the right. Cross over a bridge and continue straight ahead along pathway. Pass through a kissing gate and turn left. After about 20 yards/metres (just before a bridge) turn right and cross a stile. Continue straight ahead along path, retracing steps along riverbank and back into Uckfield.*

Access by bus and train
To Uckfield by bus from Lewes and East Grinstead and also by train from London.

Refreshments
At Ye Maidens Head or the Chalk and Cheese pubs in Uckfield or a picnic along the route.

Fishing on the River Uck

24

Barcombe

Outline
Barcombe − Delves Farm − River Ouse − Barcombe Mills − Barcombe.

Summary

AREA PRONE TO SEVERE FLOODING AFTER HEAVY RAIN! In dry weather, though, this fairly involved, yet very relaxing walk through the beautiful Sussex lowlands makes an ideal choice for a family outing. From the village of Barcombe the route cuts first through lush rolling farmland to Delves Farm in Anchor Lane, before turning back, through more fields and over a disused railway line to join the lazily meandering River Ouse. A leisurely, winding walk follows along the river bank, before the route eventually passes Barcombe Mills Station, ideally situated for well-earned refreshment, some of the 'regulars' there being an unusual collection of papier-mâché statues, including a Rasta-man with dreadlocks and a punk rocker with a pink Mohican hairstyle. A short climb follows, with a view of the South Downs to the left, before finally returning to the village.

Attractions
At the start of the walk, near Barcombe, the scene is set with a lovely view of a reservoir, perhaps with ducks bobbing on its surface and sheep grazing on the green grass of its banks. Moving on beneath a canopy of beautiful ash trees, mature oaks and spreading horse chestnuts, the route crosses the first of several lovely wooden footbridges, which, although perhaps requiring supervision, should prove a delight for children. By now the richness of this very special part of Sussex will be indelibly printed, like a detailed, colourful painting, on the eager visitor's mind. In early summer copious splashes of pink herb robert, forgetmenots, buttercups and delicate blue speedwell light up the grasses beside the pathways, while honeysuckle and dogrose hug the hedgerows and crimson poppies shine like lanterns in green fields of corn. Although extra care should be taken of younger children, the mood, perhaps inspired by the peace and natural beauty, will continue as the route drifts along the River Ouse where electric blue damsel flies flit about in the sun and where the water reflects the overhanging beech, alder and willow trees along its banks. A lane with no less than five bridges in quick succession comes next, the fourth bridge of particular interest. A plaque records that it is built on the site where a toll gate stood in 1066, the first known point at which tolls were levied in Sussex.

    The mills that once stood by the river, so alluring that artists reputedly flocked there from all over the country to try to capture their beauty on canvas, were sadly destroyed by fire in 1939, the name Barcombe Mills now applying to the area. Gone too is the railway, although the station remains, now a splendid restaurant and tea room and also where bicycles can be hired.

Route 5

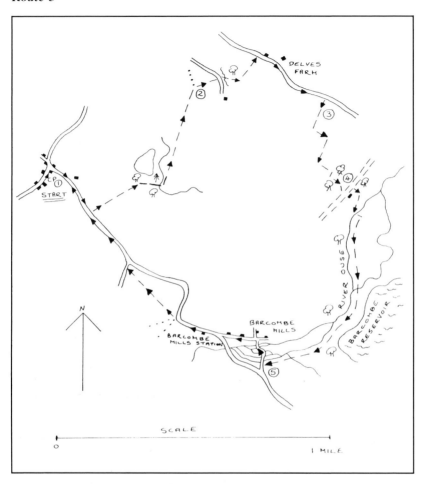

Route 5

Barcombe   4 miles

Start

At the car park in High Street (OS Pathfinder 1289 GR 421159 – opposite Barcombe Village Hall), which is a continuation of Spithurst Road, approached by the A26, A272 or A275.

Route

1. *Turn right out of car park into High Street. After about 20 yards/metres turn right into Barcombe Mills Road. Continue along road (CAUTION), passing East Lodge on the left. After about a further 200 yards/metres cross over a stile on the left into indicated footpath. Proceed downhill along right border of a field. Cross over a stile and continue downhill along indicated path between fences. At the bottom of the hill climb over a stile beside a gate and proceed along right border of a field. Cross over a wooden footbridge and then turn left, proceeding for about 100 yards/metres along bank of stream. Cross over a stile and then proceed along right border of a field. Continue as path bears slightly left through field.*

2. *Cross over a stile beside a gate and then proceed uphill through a field diagonally towards the right, in direction of yellow arrow. Cross over a stile and turn left at a lane (CAUTION). After only about 10 yards/metres turn right over a small footbridge and then cross over a stile. Proceed uphill along left border of a field. Cross over another stile and, bearing slightly left, proceed along left border of another field. Cross over a stile and turn right at a lane (CAUTION). Proceed along winding lane, passing Delves Farm on the left. Continue downhill along lane for several hundred yards/metres before crossing a stile on the right into indicated footpath.*

3. *Proceed along right border of a field. Turn left in far corner, continuing along border of same field. Pass through a gap in a hedge and then turn right, proceeding along right border of another field. Turn left in far corner, continuing along border of same field. After about 50 yards/metres pass through a gap in a hedge on the right and then turn immediately left, proceeding along left border of another field. Turn right in far corner, continuing along border of same field. After about 20 yards/metres cross a stile on the left, proceeding through a small band of dense woodland.*

4. *Turn left at stone-covered track (disused railway) and after about 10 yards/metres turn right and cross over a stile. Proceed along path beneath trees, continuing as path then leads across a small open space. Turn right, as indicated by yellow arrow, and proceed along tarmac track. After about 100 yards/metres turn left and*

Continued on page 28

27

cross over a bridge (access onto bridge, which has a gate across it, is via a small wooden platform to the right of the gate and then over a low rail on the side). Turn immediately right (in direction of footpath sign) and then cross a stile beside another gate. Follow path along river bank (CAUTION – DEEP WATER), eventually crossing over a wooden footbridge. Continue along bank of river, eventually crossing a stile and then continuing along river bank. Cross over another wooden footbridge and, bearing slightly right, continue along river bank. Cross another stile and continue along river bank.

5. *On reaching a lane turn right (CAUTION), continuing over five bridges in quick succession. On reaching an intersection turn left. Proceed along lane, continuing straight ahead as it leads into a path running beside a road. Continue (CAUTION) as path joins road, proceeding uphill past Barcombe Mills Station. After about a further 100 yards/metres cross over a stile on the left and take indicated footpath to the right, proceeding uphill through a field. Cross over a stile and proceed through another field in direction of yellow arrow. Cross over another stile, proceed through a small field and cross over yet another stile. Turn right into a lane (CAUTION). After about 50 yards/metres turn left into Barcombe Mills Road and continue back into Barcombe.*

Access by bus
To Barcombe from Lewes.

Refreshments
At Barcombe Mill Station, The Anglers Rest, or the Royal Oak in Barcombe.

Punk rocker at Barcombe Mills Station tea rooms and restaurant

28

Upper Dicker

Outline
Upper Dicker − Raylands Farm − Michelham Priory − Upper Dicker.

Summary
From the small, pretty village of Upper Dicker this route begins with a relaxing easy descent through lush green farmland to the River Cuckmere. As parents perhaps appreciate a series of stunning views over the long line of the South Downs, children will enjoy the first of many stiles and little wooden footbridges, as well as being able to keep a lookout for squirrels, rabbits and a host of farm animals along the way. Then, as the route swings round and winds its way back towards Upper Dicker, there is the chance to visit the beautiful former Augustinian priory of Michelham. Encircled by the River Cuckmere, which forms one of the largest moats in the country and at the same time powers a working watermill, the setting is idyllic, perfect not only for sightseeing, but also for well-earned refreshment, whether at the lovely priory restaurant or a picnic on a bench at the waterside.

Attractions
Although the area has plenty of natural beauty to offer throughout the seasons, a particularly lovely time is May, when the fields are speckled with blue speedwell and rich yellow buttercups and when copious displays of white hawthorn blossom decorate the hedgerows and sections of the river banks like huge canopies of lace.

Lovely views over neat, yet irregularly-shaped hedgerowed fields and rolling hills are plentiful − through a pair of binoculars during the early part of the walk the Long Man of Wilmington can be picked out quite clearly on a hillside in the distance, its origin and date debatable, yet its size (230 feet high) making it without doubt one of the largest representations of a man in the world. A mixture of open fields, shady, secluded sections of woodland, ponds, streams and the magnificent meandering River Cuckmere all add up to an outing of great variety and interest.

And then of course there is the unforgettable Michelham Priory. Built by Gilbert de Aquila in 1229, with the gatehouse added in 1385, it is now lovingly cared for by the Sussex Archaeological Society, who have made it their business to provide an almost endless list of attractions for visitors. On display are items of furniture, tapestries, musical instruments and toys and there is also a blacksmith and wheelwright's museum. Many special events are held there too, including what is reputedly the best craft fair in England. Country lunches and traditional teas are served, with cakes and bread made from their own flour which is ground in their own watermill. Local ale, apple juice, and Sussex wines are also on sale.

Back in Upper Dicker the Village Shop could be good news for youngsters in an 'ice cream frame of mind' or The Plough, with its picturesque garden and swings, might prove the ideal way to end the day.

Route 6

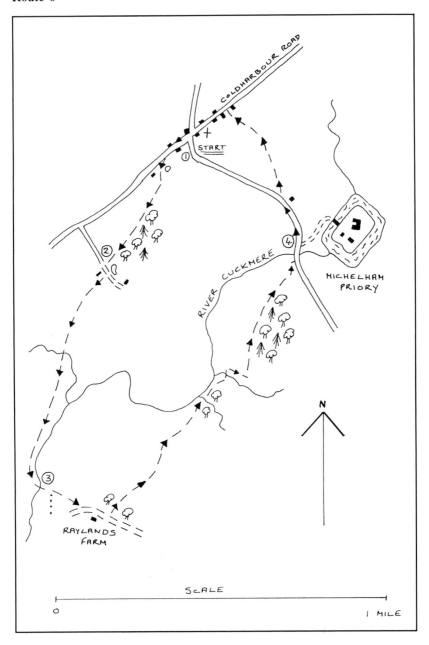

Route 6

Upper Dicker   3½ miles

Start

*In Upper Dicker at junction of Coldharbour Road and signposted turnoff to
Michelham Priory (opposite St Bede's School) (OS Pathfinder 1308 GR 551097),
approached by the A22. Limited parking near junction or in the village. Parking
is also available at Michelham Priory for visitors who purchase tickets to enter the
priory. In this case the circular walk would begin by turning right out of car park
entrance into lane and then following the route instructions from number 4.*

Route

1. *Walk along Coldharbour Road in direction of signpost towards Berwick, Alfriston
   and Seaford (CAUTION). Just past The Plough cross over a stile on the left into
   indicated Wealdway (WW). Bearing slightly right cross through a small field in
   direction of yellow arrow. Cross over another stile and proceed along right
   boundary of another field. After about 20 yards/metres cross over a stile on the
   right beside a gate. Continue along right border of a field. Pass through a gateway
   and continue along right border of a section of St Bede's Golf Course. Cross over
   a stile and continue along indicated Wealdway, with woods on the left.*

2. *Cross a stile beside a gate and turn left on reaching a track. After about 20 yards/
   metres cross over a stile on the right and cross through the middle of a field in
   direction of yellow arrow. Cross over a stile and, bearing slightly left, cross
   through another field in direction of yellow arrow. Cross over a stile and continue
   straight ahead through another field. Cross over a wooden footbridge (CAUTION)
   and, bearing slightly left cross through a long field. Cross over a stile beside a
   gate and, bearing slightly left, follow path beside river (River Cuckmere).*

3. *Cross over a stile and, almost immediately, turn left over a wooden footbridge.
   Continue uphill along winding gravel path, ignoring a stile to the right. Proceed
   straight ahead as gravel path leads into a track. After about a further 100 yards/
   metres turn left into indicated footpath to Michelham. Cross over a stile and
   proceed straight ahead in direction of yellow arrow through a field. Cross over
   another stile and bear right, following right-hand border of a field. Continue
   around border of field in direction of yellow arrows. Cross over a stile and proceed
   along right border of another field in direction of another arrow. Cross over
   another stile and proceed through a band of woods in direction of yellow arrow.
   Cross over a small footbridge and continue along left boundary of a field in
   direction of yellow arrow (beside River Cuckmere – CAUTION, high bank). Cross
   over a small farm track and then almost immediately afterwards turn left over a
   small footbridge followed by a stile. Turn right and proceed along right border of*

Continued on page 32

another field. On reaching a gate in the corner, turn left, continuing along border of same field, with woods on the right. Pass through a gateway and continue along right border of another field. Pass through another gateway and bear right along border of another field. On reaching yet another gate turn left and after only about 10 yards/metres cross a stile on the right into a lane (CAUTION). Turn left along lane and cross over a bridge.

4. *Proceed uphill along lane (past Michelham Priory entrance) and after about 200 yards/metres cross over a stile on the right (indicated by footpath sign to Hailsham). Cross through a field in direction of yellow arrow. Cross over a stile and then through another field in direction of yellow arrow. Cross over yet another stile and proceed straight ahead through yet another field. Cross another stile and follow narrow path between houses to reach village shop. Continue to Coldharbour Road and turn left to reach junction of Coldharbour Road and signposted turnoff to Michelham Priory.*

Access by bus
To Upper Dicker from Hailsham and Seaford.

Refreshments
At The Plough or perhaps a picnic.

Gatehouse to Michelham Priory over moat (River Cuckmere)

Alfriston

Outline
Alfriston − Lullington Church − Litlington − Alfriston.

Summary
"Help a toad to cross the road" − one of the more unusual road signs that might be seen in and around the small hamlet of Litlington near Alfriston, a sign that not only advises of the toad migration in spring, but is also an indication of the depth of concern by local people for the 'lesser' creatures that share their environment. Children and parents alike shouldn't have any doubt about the sincerity of the sentiment either, as they stroll from the picturesque riverside village of Alfriston through the beautiful surrounding farmland. A further sign asks motorists to drive slowly in case of cats on the road, while swans gliding gracefully along the river and horses, cattle and sheep grazing peacefully in lush green pastues are a picture of contentment. Visitors will also be able to see what is probably the smallest church in England, on a hill at Lullington, its little white belfry visible in the distance once again on the relaxing walk back to Alfriston along the gently meandering River Cuckmere.

Attractions
The smuggling days of the 18th and 19th centuries are what immediately spring to mind for most people visiting Alfriston, although human habitation in the area actually goes back as far as Prehistoric times. Stanton Collins, the leader of the notorious Alfriston Gang, used to live in Market Cross House, which is now known simply as The Smugglers Inn, an ideal building for the purpose with its six staircases and a number of cleverly-concealed emergency exits in many of the rooms. Sadly for him though such ingenuity was not enough to save him from being transported in 1831 for receiving stolen goods. Another hang out for the gangsters, who exploited the potential of nearby Cuckmere Haven for their illicit activities, was the Star Inn, dating from around 1420, an establishment first used by pilgrims. Many other old buildings in the town provide a further insight into life in those early times, not least of which is the 15th century Old Forge Heritage Centre and Blacksmiths Museum. Another very famous building is the Old Clergy House, with interesting views both of the part-thatched, part-tiled roof at the back, seen from the riverbank, and also the timber beams and neat entrance seen from beside the churchyard in the front. Originally a priest's house in about 1350, it was the first house acquired by the National Trust, its price in 1896 a snip at £10.

Across the River Cuckmere on the side of a hill is the recently restored Plonk Barn, which was built in 1698, and on top of the hill is the 16 foot-square Lullington Church, its name derived from a medieval group of settlers known as Lulla's people. The views from the churchyard towards Alfriston in the valley below and the surrounding rolling

Continued on page 36

Route 7

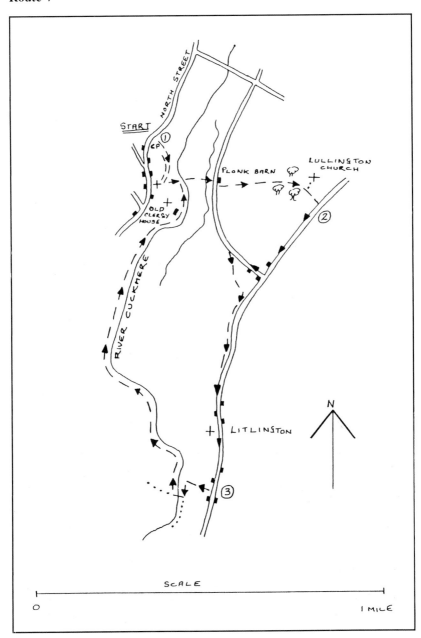

Route 7

Alfriston   2½ miles

Start
From The Willows Car and Coach Park in North Street (OS Pathfinder 1308 GR 521033), approached by A27.

Route
1. *Take indicated footpath to the river from the rear right-hand corner of the car park. After about 20 yards/metres cross a stile and proceed along farm track. Cross a second stile and continue along track towards church. Just in front of church turn left along tarmac path and cross the river via a footbridge (The White Bridge). Continue straight ahead along footpath between hedges. Cross a second footbridge and then cross over a lane (CAUTION), passing through an indicated gate to Lullington Church just to the right of Plonk Barn. Continue up a series of wooden steps and pass through a second gate. Continue uphill along a path and then continue straight ahead along left border of a field in direction of sign to church. Cross a stile and continue through a small band of woods. Turn left at indicated footpath to see Lullington Church. Return to main path and turn left, continuing downhill to reach a lane.*

2. *Turn right at the lane (CAUTION). After several hundred yards/metres turn right again into indicated lane towards Alfriston. After about 200 yards/metres turn left into indicated South Downs Way. After a short distance cross a stile and proceed straight ahead through a field. Cross another stile and bear left, following path around the border of another field. Cross a further stile and follow a path running parallel to a lane. As path joins the lane continue downhill through Litlington.*

3. *Just before The Plough and Harrow pub turn right along indicated footpath. Continue downhill and then bear left at the river. After about 50 yards/metres turn right over a footbridge. Turn sharp right again immediately after the bridge and after 20 yards/metres cross over a stile. Follow winding path along bank of the river all the way back to Alfriston, eventually retracing steps to car park from The White Bridge.*

Access by bus
To Alfriston from Brighton, Seaford and Eastbourne.

downland is quite breathtaking, with more lovely open scenery on all sides as the route approaches Litlington, its own church dating back to about 1150.

The route could be extended by continuing downstream for about half a mile from Litlington and then doubling back at the next footbridge and some walkers might even consider carrying on for several miles to the Seven Sisters Country Park at the coast. Others may prefer to go there by car afterwards, perhaps stopping in at The Living World, an insect and shorelife exhibition in a barn opposite the main car park. A visit might also be made to Drusillas Zoo, just north of Alfriston, ideal for children, with an adventure playground and a railway journey through animal paddocks.

Refreshments
At Litlington Tea Gardens and Nursery or one of many lovely pubs and tea shops in Alfriston. Or perhaps a picnic at the site beside the car park.

Swan on River Cuckmere at The White Bridge

Birling Gap (Seven Sisters Cliff)

Outline
Birling Gap — Seven Sisters Cliff — Crowlink House — Birling Gap.

Summary
Passing mainly through the National Trust Crowlink, which sits astride four of the famous Seven Sisters, this walk is simply spectacular. From the small, yet pretty settlement of Birling Gap, landing point for smugglers in the 18th and early 19th centuries, the route runs up and down the steep slopes along the clifftop. The fresh smell of the sea and the sound of the waves lapping on the shore far below combine almost magically with the far-reaching views along the coastline ahead and the openness of the Downs away to the side, making it an exhilarating outing. For the very energetic the walk could be extended by continuing along the clifftop into the Seven Sisters Country Park, although for parents, who should keep a tight hold on youngsters, the turn to the right leading inland might come as a relief, a chance at last to let the children safely run about to their hearts content, with the prospect of many delights yet to come.

Attractions
Through a pair of binoculars the white face of the Seven Sisters Cliff may appear to be in a constant state of movement. And of course, in a geological sense it is, since its very existence is the result of constant maritime erosion. More immediately, though, the impression is likely to be attributable to a mass of wheeling birds in the air, dozens of gigantic well-fed seagulls and the smaller grey-crowned jackdaws, which like to nest in the chalky crevices. Countless burrows along the clifftop are evidence of the many rabbits in the area too, although the little creatures themselves are so swift that the only sight of them may be the flash of a tail bobbing away into hiding. Whole flocks of downland sheep, on the other hand, are not so easily missed, even without their almost raucous bleating and in springtime, in the fields just below the beautiful flint-walled Crowlink House, where smuggled gin known as 'Genuine Crowlink' was reputedly stored, the sight of new-born lambs struggling to find their shaky legs will have most visitors, especially children, absolutely enthralled. Also in spring, the pink-breasted chaffinch might be seen, perhaps perched on a twig in a hedgerow or thicket, heralding the new season with its sharp intermittent call, so different from one of its neighbours, the skylark, seen nosing in and out of the grasses or hovering in the sky, its own song, an unmistakeable persistent trilling, sometimes lasting for up to five minutes at a time.

An interesting feature on the clifftop is the Sarsen Stone which was erected by The Society of Sussex Downmen in appreciation of the generosity of William Charles Campbell. It was thanks to a large donation from him that led to the purchase of the

Continued on page 40

Route 8

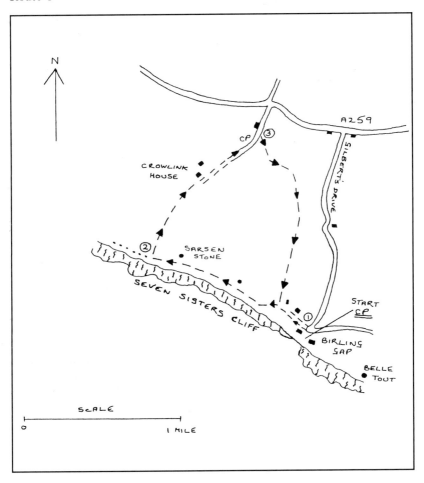

Route 8

Birling Gap (Seven Sisters Cliff) 3½ miles

Start

> At the car park beside the Birling Gap Hotel (OS Landranger 199 GR 554960) at
> the bottom of Birling Gap Road, which is a continuation of Gilberts Drive off
> the A259.

Route

1. With Birling Gap Hotel on your left, leave car park through main entrance and
   turn left. Proceed through a gate uphill along a track indicated by footpath arrows.
   At the top of the hill continue along indicated South Downs Way. After about
   20 yards/metres bear left, continuing along South Downs Way. Pass through a gate
   into National Trust Crowlink and follow pathway along Seven Sisters Cliff
   (CAUTION – CLIFF EDGE), continuing past the First World War Memorial and
   the Sarsen Stone.

2. At the bottom of the slope just beyond the Sarsen Stone turn right and proceed
   inland along a grassy pathway. Continue along path in direction of a signpost to
   Friston. On reaching a wooden gate bear right and follow a path beside a
   hedgerow. Pass through a small gate and continue along the path. Pass through
   a second gate and proceed along a dirt track, which leads into a tarmac lane.
   Follow lane up a long, gently sloping hill. Continue through a car park.

3. Just beyond the car park turn right through a gate and then bear right along a path
   indicated by a yellow arrow. Pass through a kissing gate and turn left. Proceed
   along the boundary of a field before passing through a second kissing gate in the
   direction of a yellow arrow. Continue along a grassy path, which leads first beside
   a stone wall and then bears slowly towards the right through an open field. Pass
   through a gate into a signposted path to Birling Gap. Pass through a second gate
   and retrace steps to car park.

Access by bus
To Birling Gap from Eastbourne and Seaford.

Crowlink Valley for the use and enjoyment of the nation. There is a bench nearby with a stunning view of the coastline. Towards the end of the walk, as the route eventually begins its gentle homeward descent, a further quick succession of breathtaking panoramas still lies deliciously in wait. Passing through a wooden kissing gate the path runs beneath a small clump of trees (a welcome patch of shade on a hot summer's day) and beyond a small stone wall to the left the old village of East Dean can be seen far below on the valley floor, backed by rolling hills with their patchwork of delightfully varied colours. Not long afterwards the sea comes into view again over to the right, with the lonely Belle Tout lighthouse (its light long since removed to Beachy Head) on a hilltop in the distance straight ahead. And then suddenly Birling Gap can be seen again, a small clutch of buildings in the valley, flanked by steeply rising slopes and, on a sunny day, the twinkling surface of the sea beside it, a far cry perhaps from cold misty nights when smugglers brought ashore their contraband of tea, perfume, spirits and lace from the Continent.

Refreshments
At the Birling Gap Hotel or a picnic on the nearby slopes.

Seven Sisters Cliff

Windmill Hill and Herstmonceux Castle

Outline
Windmill Hill − Herstmonceux Castle − Plantation Wood − Windmill Hill.

Summary
From Windmill Hill on the busy A271 this route at first follows the peaceful Comphurst Lane, which is lined with a beautiful variety of trees, including oaks, ash, alders, beech, poplars and silver birch, together with abundant outcrops of mixed hedgerows, the air fragrant in early summer with the scent of white and crimson dogrose and, later, with clusters of sweet golden honeysuckle. Then suddenly the relative cosiness of this natural tunnel opens out with breathtaking views of Herstmonceux Place towards the right and, in the distance ahead, the long line of the Sussex Downs behind Beachy Head. Linking up with a bridleway (uneven ground and muddy after rain!) the route moves on through more lovely woods, their welcome, cooling shade providing delicious refreshment on a hot sunny day, and then, quite dramatically, the magnificent red-bricked Herstmonceux Castle comes into view. Moving closer and then around the front, an ideal vantage point is reached, the two red turrets, fronted by a long bridge over a moat, making a perfect postcard picture, the sort that children might later want to sketch, from memory perhaps or a photograph or one similar in many a favourite storybook. Through more woods and then again more open fields, the route leads back to Comphurst Lane and to Windmill Hill, perhaps in time for a drink or a meal at the very attractive Horse Shoe Inn.

Attractions
In the days of the infamous Alfriston Gang, who reputedly used the then abandoned Herstmonceux Castle as a store for their smuggled goods, locals in the area lived in mortal dread of a nine-foot headless drummer who apparently patrolled the battlements at night. Invented by the smugglers themselves to keep their nosy neighbours at bay, it was one of many similar chilling stories created for that same purpose throughout the country. Less gruesome perhaps, although just as interesting is the rest of the castle's history, the only red-bricked castle in Sussex, complete with a window for every day of the year and a chimney for every Sunday. Built in the 15th century with Flemish bricks, it was commissioned by the De Monceux family who came to England from Normandy with William the Conqueror. During the 18th century the castle fell into disrepair and then in 1948 it was taken over by the Royal Greenwich Observatory, with the subsequent erection nearby of six steel and copper domes and a telescope. The observatory has since moved to Cambridge and the castle has once again undergone restoration. Access to the gardens and parkland is available to the public.

Throughout the route an even mixture of open areas and shady woods make the

Continued on page 44

Route 9

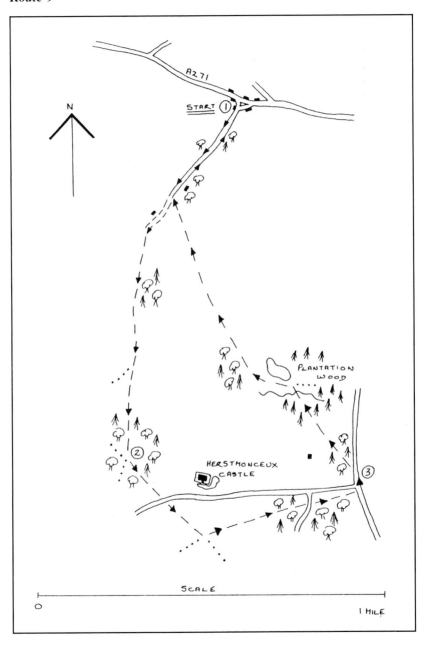

42

Route 9

Windmill Hill and Herstmonceux Castle   3½ miles

Start

> At Comphurst Lane in Windmill Hill beside the Horse Shoe Inn (OS Pathfinder 1290 GR 649120), approached by the A271. Limited parking near pub or in village.

Route

1. From Horse Shoe Inn walk down Comphurst Lane, indicated by yellow arrow and sign to Comphurst and Little Comphurst. Proceed to end of lane, continuing straight ahead as it leads into a dirt track. After a further 50 yards/metres climb over a stile beside a gate and continue downhill as track leads into a footpath. Continue along winding footpath, eventually passing through a gate indicated by blue arrow. Proceed straight ahead along right border of a field, eventually passing through a gate and continuing along a track in direction of blue arrow. After about 50 yards/metres bear slightly left along a bridleway leading uphill through a field in direction of blue arrow. At the top of the hill pass through a gate and continue through a small band of woods along bridleway indicated by blue arrow. Pass through another gate and continue through woods.

2. On reaching an indicated intersection of paths, take footpath to the left. After about 50 yards/metres cross a stile and continue straight ahead along indicated footpath through a field. Climb over a stile, cross over a driveway and continue along indicated footpath between wooden fences. After about 20 yards/metres cross over a stile and proceed through a field in direction of footpath sign. On reaching another indicated intersection of paths, take the bridleway to the left. After about 50 yards/metres pass through a gate and follow indicated bridleway uphill between fences. Pass through another gate and continue uphill along bridleway, which then leads through woods. Cross over a driveway and continue along bridleway through woods.

3. On reaching a road turn left (CAUTION). After about 50 yards/metres cross over a stile on the left and follow indicated footpath through a field. Cross over a stile and proceed downhill through woods in direction of yellow arrow. Cross over a small footbridge at the bottom of the hill and continue past a pond along path through woods. Cross over a stile and turn left along a bridleway. Pass through a gate and continue straight ahead through a field. Pass through another gate and follow bridleway uphill through another field. Turn right into Comphurst Lane and retrace steps to car.

Access by bus

To Windmill Hill from Hastings and Eastbourne.

going both comfortable and fascinating. With nesting rooks in late spring shrieking from their lofty perches, little wrens twittering in the hedgerows and fleeting swifts shooting through the air, with pretty red campions, buttercups, white stitchwort and wild purple rhododendrons, with rabbits darting away into bushes, with sheep, cattle, horses and even perhaps the odd goat grazing happily in the lovely meadows and with regular stunning views over folding fields and hazy-blue rolling hills, there is bound to be something to delight every member of the family.

An additional attraction is a chance perhaps after the walk to visit The Truggery, just to the west of the village of Herstmonceux on the A271. Invented by the Smith family the trug is a traditional wooden basket used by gardeners, which first became popular in the mid 19th century.

Refreshments
At the Horse Shoe Inn or perhaps a picnic on the walk.

Herstmonceux Castle

44

Punnett's Town

Outline
Punnett's Town − Blackdown Mill (Cherry Black) − Three Cups Corner − Punnett's Town.

Summary
Lovely views from the top of North Street, the striking picture of the gleaming white Blackdown Mill, are just a few of the many delights to be found in and around the little village of Punnett's Town. Yet be warned, with a large number of extremely high and sometimes very tricky stiles and with several sections of the walk tending to have rather uneven ground, which turns to mud after rain, this must rate as one of the more difficult routes in our selection, a reminder perhaps that although some of the best things in life are undoubtedly free, they are not always necessarily easy.

Attractions
Rudyard Kipling called the Punnett's Town mill the 'Cherry Black Windmill'. And, as many children and their parents may already know, he featured it in many of his stories. Towering majestically on a hilltop with its white frame and huge sails almost blinding on a sunny day, its real name is the Blackdown Mill, although it is also known as 'Cherry Clack'. Once sited amongst the cherry orchards in Biddenden it was transported to Punnett's Town in pieces by cart and was erected in 1856 by Stephen Neve of Rushlake Green. The mill wore out and stopped working in 1928 and was later used as a store for cattle feed. Its current splendour is thanks to William Dallaway who decided to restore it.

At various points throughout the walk 'Cherry Black' can be seen in the distance, perhaps on the downhill stroll from Three Cups Corner, through a gap in a mixed hedgerow of honeysuckle, hawthorn, hazel and holly, or as the route heads back towards Punnett's Town, the visitor's direction confirmed by the sudden sighting of its white sails on a hill across the valley slightly towards the right, the view across miles of farmland to the left bounded by the distinctive sculpture of the South Downs.

Throughout the walk there is something of interest for all ages in the family, although in the early part of the route along the quiet village lanes some of the quaint and beautiful cottages might possibly result in the odd twinge of envy amongst the parents, the well-kept and obviously well-loved gardens simply idyllic. Children too might find themselves wishing that they could live in the country, especially on a farm, as they come across the many farm animals along the way. How special when a lamb looks up and wags its tail, what depth of patience and innocence in the eyes of a silently watching cow, what surprise and laughter as a chicken squawks in panic and scurries away!

Route 10

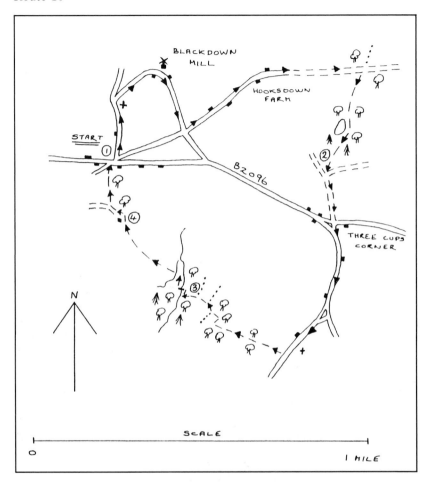

Route 10

Punnett's Town   3 miles

Start

At the corner of North Street and the B2096 (OS Pathfinder 1270 GR 626204). Limited parking beside B2096 and in North Street or village.

Route

1. *From B2096 proceed uphill along North Street. On reaching a fork at the top of the hill turn right. Proceed uphill all the way to the windmill. Continue along lane over the brow of the hill and then down the other side. On reaching an intersection of lanes turn left. Continue along lane, passing first Hooksdown Farm on the right and then Watkins Down Riding School on the left. Continue straight ahead as lane eventually leads into a dirt track. Follow dirt track for several hundred yards/ metres before turning right into a bridleway beside a gate. Proceed along path between fences, passing a pond on the right (MUDDY AFTER RAIN).*

2. *On eventually reaching a small intersection of tracks take second track on the left to reach a road. Cross over road (CAUTION) and proceed along short slip-road directly opposite. Turn left into a lane (CAUTION) and proceed downhill. On reaching a fork keep to the right (in direction of signpost to Hailsham). Continue downhill and after a further several hundred yards/metres (just past Mount Hermon Baptist Chapel) cross over a partially-concealed stile on the right. Follow path along left border of a field (UNEVEN GROUND). Cross over a stile and proceed along left border of another field. Cross over another stile and follow path through a small band of woods. Cross over another stile and proceed straight ahead through a field. Cross over another stile, then follow path as it swings first right and then almost immediately left through trees (can be overgrown with bracken in summer!). On reaching an intersecting path turn right. Follow path downhill, ignoring a stile on the right. Cross over a stile halfway down the hill and continue downhill along right border of a field.*

3. *Cross over a stile in the bottom corner of field into indicated footpath straight ahead (ignore stile on the right). Proceed downhill into woods and after only about 20 yards/metres turn right along indicated footpath beside a stream. After about 10 yards/metres cross over stream via stepping stones (in direction of yellow arrow). Cross over a stile and then turn right, following right border of a field. Cross over a stile in the corner, then cross over another stile immediately on the left. Step across a small stream and proceed uphill through a field. Pass through a gateway (or over stile beside it) in top left corner of field and continue uphill along left border of another field. Cross over stile in top left corner and continue uphill along left border of yet another field. Pass through (or over) a gate in top left corner.* Continued on page 48

47

4. *Continue uphill for about 20 yards/metres (beside farmhouse) and then turn left. After about another 20 yards/metres turn right into farm driveway. After a further 50 yards/metres (as driveway swings to the left) cross through (or over) a gate straight ahead and follow right border of a field as indicated by yellow arrow. Cross over a stile in top right corner of field to join road leading to B2096. Turn right and retrace steps to car.*

Access by bus
To Punnett's Town from Heathfield.

Refreshments
At the Barley Mow pub in Punnett's Town or The Three Cups Inn.

Blackdown Mill

48

Wood's Corner

Outline

Wood's Corner — The Sugar Loaf Folly — Deer Park Wood — The Observatory — Brightling Down — Wood's Corner.

Summary

Was Mad Jack Fuller really mad? And was he really the honest, fine upstanding member of society, the sympathetic benefactor of the poor, that he would by all accounts have everyone believe? Mad or not, it appeared to be generally accepted that he was an eccentric who was clearly rather partial to architectural indulgences, one of them being The Brightling Needle to the north of Wood's Corner on the turnoff to Brightling. As to his honesty, visitors might perhaps guess for themselves as they pass two of his other creations on this route, first The Sugar Loaf Folly and then later The Observatory. What precisely was the main purpose of that observatory? And was the hasty erection of The Sugar Loaf Folly the action of an honourable man? What too was his interest in Birling Gap, an interest that led him to build the Belle Tout Lighthouse?

Attractions

It was Mad Jack Fuller's respected wish to be buried in a sitting position wearing a top hat and clutching a bottle of wine, beneath a pyramid of his own design in Brightling churchyard. In those days his house, which is now known as Brightling Park, was called Rose Hill. The story goes that Jack, always an outspoken man, rashly made a bet one day that the church in Dallington, a hamlet to the south, could be seen from Rose Hill. When he discovered to his horror on arriving home that this wasn't in fact the case, he quickly built The Sugar Loaf Folly from which it was actually possible to see the church — fast thinking that not only won him the bet but also saved him from being branded a liar!

Another of Mad Jack's fervent claims, or Squire John as he was also known to some, presumably depending on their disposition to the man, was that the erection of The Observatory was purely and simply to further his interest in astronomy. Rather than make any unjust accusations, those with faith must assume that the view commanded by the building of a long section of the coast and the fact that this made it ideal as a signalling station were nothing more than coincidence. Further, it should in that case be assumed that the Belle Tout Lighthouse, hardly ideal as a lighthouse since it was fogbound for six months of the year, although arguably very handy at times for smugglers landing at Birling Gap, was just another one of those perfectly blameless things. No doubt too, all the hollow follies that were erected along recognised smugglers' routes, where the coast runners passed their goods over to the inland smugglers for transportation into London, were in truth merely follies.

Continued on page 52

Route 11

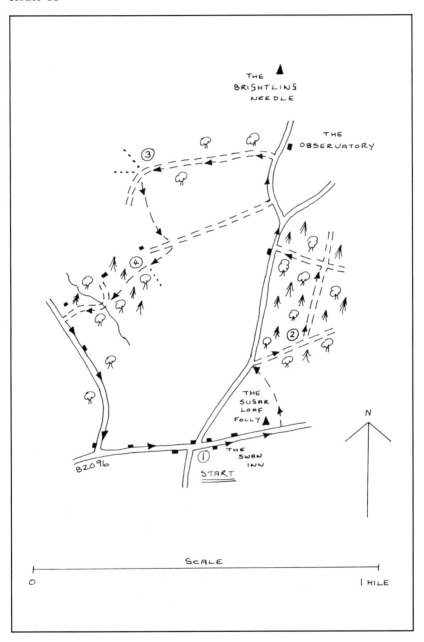

THE
BRIGHTLINS
NEEDLE

THE
OBSERVATORY

③

④

②

THE
SUGAR
LOAF
FOLLY

N

B2096

THE
SWAN
INN

①

START

SCALE

O   1 MILE

50

Route 11

Wood's Corner   3½ miles

Start

*At The Swan Inn in Wood's Corner (corner of B2096 and turn-off to Brightling —
OS Pathfinder 1290 GR 667195). Limited parking near corner or in village.*

Route

1. *With The Swan Inn on the right proceed along B2096 (CAUTION), passing
   Fuller's Cottages on the left. (The Sugar Loaf Folly can be reached via a short path
   leading through a gate from the B2096.) About 50 yards/metres beyond the gate
   leading to The Sugar Loaf Folly turn left through another gateway into indicated
   public footpath. Proceed straight ahead through a field in direction of sign (VERY
   UNEVEN GROUND). Pass through a gateway and follow path downhill between
   fences (GROUND STILL UNEVEN). At the bottom of the hill turn left along a
   driveway. On reaching a road turn immediately right, passing through a gap
   beside a gate leading into indicated Deer Park Wood. Continue straight ahead
   along wide grassy track.*

2. *After several hundred yards/metres turn left along track leading uphill through
   trees. On reaching an intersection of tracks turn left, continuing to reach a road.
   Turn right and proceed along road (CAUTION). After about 100 yards/metres turn
   left along road in direction of sign towards Burwash and Batemans. Continue
   uphill along road and just before reaching The Observatory turn left, then pass
   through a gap beside a gateway. Continue along a track which leads past a raised
   reservoir on the right. Proceed downhill along track, passing through another gap
   beside another gateway. Continue downhill along track.*

3. *On reaching an intersection of paths and tracks turn left along grassy pathway
   leading along side of hill. Cross over a stile and proceed straight ahead through
   a field in direction of yellow arrow (UNEVEN GROUND). Pass through a gap in
   a hedge, cross over a dirt track and then climb over a stile into another field.
   Bearing towards the right cross through field in direction of footpath sign.*

4. *Cross over a stile and follow path into woods. On reaching a fork (after only about
   10 yards/metres) take path to the right. Continue along path through woods. Cross
   over a stile and continue straight ahead along path. Cross over a second stile and,
   bearing slightly towards the left, continue along path which eventually leads into
   a driveway. Proceed along driveway, crossing a bridge and continuing uphill to
   eventually reach a lane. Turn left along lane, continuing to reach the B2096. Turn
   left into B2096 (CAUTION) and continue back to Wood's Corner.*

It is all so long ago that the question of Squire John's guilt or innocence in the early part of the 19th century hardly matters now, a chance rather for parents and children to chuckle as they discuss the sometimes rather debatable nature of history, while also enjoying being together as a family in the country. A mixture of woodland and open fields provides a lovely contrast along the walk and from several points, especially the high ground near The Observatory, the views are absolutely stunning, including the already mentioned coastline, which can be seen clearly with the naked eye and is full of detail, such as the white foam of breaking waves or perhaps an occasional passing ship, if looked at through a pair of binoculars. From the track leading away from The Observatory the church at Dallington can also be seen (yes, truly!), once again a good pair of binoculars doing better justice to the spectacle. Children might enjoy seeing farm animals along the way and if they are lucky perhaps even a gathering of grazing deer, while for wildflower fans there is bound to be plenty to get excited about, both in the early part of the year and throughout the summer.

Access by bus
To Wood's Corner from Heathfield and Hastings.

Refreshments
The Swan Inn in Wood's Corner.

Path leading to The Sugar Loaf Folly

Ticehurst and Bewl Water

Outline

Ticehurst — Bewl Water — Three Leg Cross — Ticehurst.

Summary

From the village of Ticehurst, which derives its name from Ticen-hurst, meaning a wooded hill where goats are fed, this walk moves northwards in a fairly straight line through a succession of rich farmland fields and a small section of woodland before reaching the great Bewl Water or Bewl Bridge Reservoir, a haven for bird-life. After following the bank of the reservoir with a series of constantly changing lovely views across the water and over the countryside on the other side, the route then swings back towards Ticehurst, passing through the quaint little hamlet of Three Leg Cross on the way.

Attractions

Bewl Water was built by the Southern Water Authority between 1972 and 1975 as part of the River Medway Scheme to supply water to parts of north and west Kent. With more than 127 acres (50 hectares) of the surrounding land leased to the Sussex Trust for Nature Conservation the area is full of bird, insect and plant-life, the diversity stimulated by a policy of using hardly any fertilizers or weed killers. A system of careful management provides a never-ending variety of species, depending on the particular point in the cycle and also the type of habitat.

The deciduous woodland, made up of sweet chestnut, oak, birch, alder, holly, hazel and hawthorn is home to many different kinds of insects, mammals and birds, especially the oak which alone provides food and shelter for over 200 species. Coppicing or wood-cutting, which takes place every 12 to 18 years, allows more sunlight to reach the ground and at this time there is an abundance of wildflowers, including bluebells, campions, wood anemones and the tall, elegant foxgloves. As the ground later becomes increasingly covered with other forms of plant-life refuge is provided for a variety of birds such as robins, thrushes, blackbirds and wrens. Animals such as foxes, hares and badgers also thrive in this environment.

The grasslands too are carefully looked after, rich at one stage with plant-life such as ox-eyed daisies, vetches, clovers and early purple orchids, the result being an increase in butterflies, their larvae provided with plenty of food. As the grass reaches full maturity it creates an ideal nesting ground for birds, for example the skylark or the meadow pipit. The area is also inhabited by little mammals like field mice and voles, which are food themselves in the sometimes seemingly cruel cycle of nature, for birds of prey such as swooping kestrels and owls.

The waterside is used as an overwintering site for many birds, including geese,

Continued on page 56

Route 12

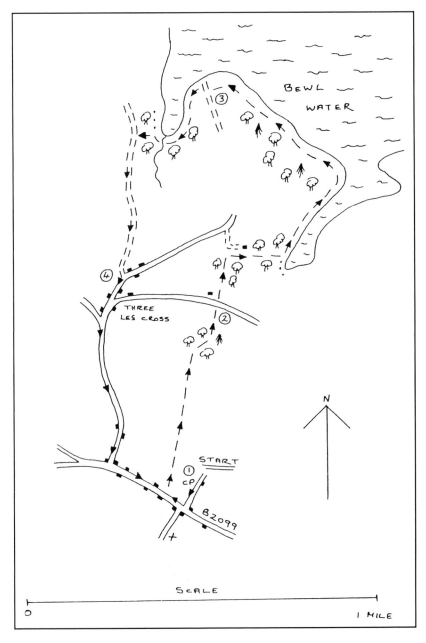

54

Route 12

Ticehurst and Bewl Water

4 miles

Start

At Ticehurst car park in Pickforde Lane (OS Pathfinder 1249 GR 689303), off High Street which is part of the B2099.

Route

1. *Turn right out of car park entrance and proceed to end of Pickforde Lane. Turn right into High Street and proceed past the Bell Hotel. After about a further hundred yards/metres turn right into indicated narrow footpath between buildings. After a further hundred yards/metres cross over a stile and continue along footpath as it leads first between fences and then along left border of a field (UNEVEN GROUND). Pass through a gap in a hedge and proceed downhill along path as it leads this time along right border of a field. Cross over a stile and proceed downhill along path between trees, continuing as it bears slightly towards the right and then after a short distance towards the left. Continue along path as it then leads uphill along left border of a field.*

2. *Cross over a lane (CAUTION) and proceed down tarmac driveway directly opposite. After about 20 yards/metres (as driveway swings to the left) continue straight ahead along indicated footpath leading downhill between fences and then uphill between trees. Just before reaching a gravel driveway turn right into bridleway also leading between trees. (Part of this next short stretch can be slightly overgrown in mid-summer and muddy after rain!) On reaching an intersection of bridleways turn left. Continue along bridleway for about ¾ mile around perimeter of Bewl Water (CAUTION – HORSES HAVE RIGHT OF WAY ON BRIDLEWAYS).*

3. *Pass through a gap beside a gate and turn right into a track (in direction of sign indicating Round Bewl Water Walk). After about 20 yards/metres turn left along pathway and continue around perimeter of Bewl Water, parts of which wind through woods on the waterside. Just after crossing a wooden bridge turn left through a gate and proceed uphill along path indicated by sign as Round Bewl Water Walk. At the top of the hill turn left into a track in direction of sign to Three Leg Cross. Continue along winding track to eventually reach a lane.*

4. *Turn right into lane (CAUTION) and proceed through Three Leg Cross, continuing as lane bears slightly towards the left just past The Bull. Follow lane all the way to its end (FAIRLY QUIET, BUT CAUTION REQUIRED). On reaching B2099 turn left into Ticehurst. Continue along High Street past the Bell Hotel and retrace steps to car park.*

ducks, divers and wading birds and at the same time is a resting point for many migrants such as wheatears, whinchats, greenshank, redshank, warblers, terns and both the common and green sandpiper. A good pair of binoculars might prove invaluable for human visitors! Ospreys have also been seen here on their long journey from Scandinavia to South Africa, while permanent residents include the great crested grebe, coots, mallards and moorhens.

Although each season offers something interesting, something special in its own way, the best time for this walk is probably on a sunny summer day when the butterflies come out and when dragonflies and delicate damselflies can be seen flitting about or settling on the plants at the waterside to deposit their eggs, the next generation, in the sparkling blue water. And perhaps on another day a visit can also be made to the Bewl Water Visitors Centre, on the north side of the reservoir in Kent, approached by the A21, where children can enjoy the adventure playground which includes a wooden ark, and where the family might enjoy a picnic or perhaps further exploration along a comprehensive network of footpaths, one of them leading the full 13 miles around the reservoir!

Access by bus
To Ticehurst from Tunbridge Wells.

Refreshments
The Chequers, the Bell Hotel, the Duke of York or The Tea Shoppe in Ticehurst or The Bull in Three Leg Cross.

Walter's Farm

56

Robertsbridge

Outline
Robertsbridge − Bugswell Farm − Squibs Farm − Robertsbridge.

Summary
Two rather different aspects combine most effectively on this route to provide the family with an outing full of fascinating variety. Along the first part of the walk progress is likely to be slow, thanks not only to a succession of frequent and sometimes fairly high stiles, as well as more than a few patches of well-hooved and therefore uneven ground (muddy too, when wet!), but also, more importantly, by a stunning display of far-reaching views in every direction. Then, on the second half of the walk, where the going for a change just couldn't be easier, the route follows a path back to Robertsbridge along the beautiful bank of a peaceful stream, which runs for a distance along the valley floor parallel to the River Rother.

Attractions
Set beside the River Rother in an area laced so liberally with streams it is hardly surprising that Robertsbridge should have taken its name from a bridge-builder. Known in the 13th century as Roberti Ponti, it was called after Robert de Martin, whose works included the founding, in 1176, of a Cistercian Abbey (now Abbey Farm) just to the east of the village. Later, in the 16th century, Robertsbridge was a major ordnance supplier and then in the 18th and early 19th centuries it became a haunt for smugglers. It is now one of the few remaining areas in Sussex to continue growing hops, a crop that used to be widespread across the county. To many, though, Robertsbridge is known first and foremost as the home of the cricket bat, the suppliers, Gray Nicholls (established in 1876), having provided the best in bats for players all over the world.

But back on the inescapable subject of bridges, this route, in keeping with the name of the village, is absolutely full of them. Children are bound to be delighted by the prospect of crossing an ingenious range from simple planks and earth mounds to more structured walled or wooden-railed footbridges, sometimes with challenging stiles at either end. In the inter-linking fields, where there is plenty of room to frolick, they can also watch out for a wide range of animals, from rabbits and sheep to cattle and horses, sometimes with their own 'youngsters' at their side.

Too close an eye, though, can hardly be kept on children as the second part of the route runs very close to the edge of a stream for some considerable distance. Having said that, this very different and much easier section of the walk has its own undeniable charm, the water bordered with alders, ash trees, hawthorn and hazel and the banks dotted with clumps of wildflowers, notably the cuckoo flower and the tall, bright yellow marsh marigolds or kingcups, with their distinctive kidney-shaped leaves.

Route 13

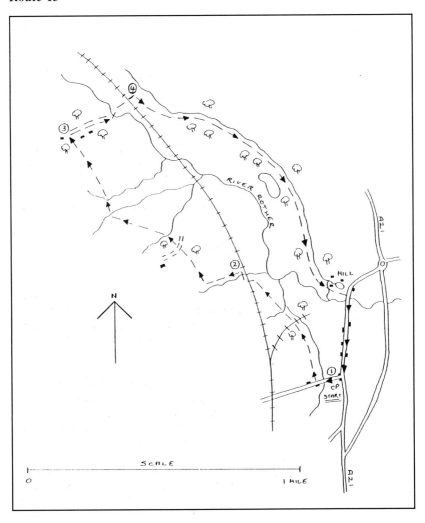

Route 13

Robertsbridge   4 miles

Start

At the Robertsbridge car park in Station Road (OS Pathfinder 1270 GR 737236) off the High Street, which is an extension of The Clappers and forms part of the A21.

Route

1. *Turn left out of car park and walk downhill along Station Road. After about 100 yards/metres (just beyond bridge) turn right into tarmac driveway of Gray Nicholls. Proceed straight ahead as driveway leads into a footpath. Continue along path beside stream. Cross over a stile beside a gate and follow path under railway bridge. Continue through a field. Cross over a small footbridge and, bearing slightly left, proceed through another field. Cross over a stile beside a gate in far left corner of field. Follow track beneath railway bridge and then cross another stile beside another gate. Turn immediately right and cross a stile, followed by a footbridge and then another stile.*

2. *Turn immediately left and follow path in direction of yellow arrow. After about 300 yards/metres cross over a stile beside a gateway and then turn right, proceeding uphill along right border of a field. Cross over a stile and continue uphill along right border of yet another field. After about a hundred yards/metres cross over a stile on the right. Turn immediately left and proceed along left border of a field. Cross a stile in far left corner of field. Cross over a track and proceed downhill along indicated footpath between fences. Cross over a small footbridge and then a stile. Bearing slightly left, cross through a field in direction of yellow arrow. Cross over a footbridge and proceed along left border of a field. Cross over a stile, then a footbridge, then a stile. Proceed uphill along left border of a field. Cross over a stile beside a gate and proceed along left border of another field.*

3. *Pass through a gate into a farmyard and after a short distance turn right into a track. Follow track downhill, eventually passing through a gate. Continue along track for a further 20 yards/metres before turning left over a concrete bridge. Pass through a gate at the end of the bridge and, bearing slightly right, cross through a field to reach a railway crossing.*

4. *Cross a stile and then with CAUTION cross over railway line. Cross another stile and turn immediately right, following indicated path beside stream. After several hundred yards/metres cross a stile and continue along path through a field. Cross another stile and continue along path beside stream, eventually passing ponds on the right. (CAUTION: path runs very close to edge of stream − keep a close eye*

Continued on page 60

59

on young children!) Continue along path, crossing another stile and then a footbridge. Proceed straight ahead through mill yard in direction of footpath sign. Turn right into road (CAUTION) and cross a bridge, continuing all the way through the village, eventually turning right into Station Road to reach Robertsbridge car park.

Access by bus and train
To Robertsbridge by bus from Battle and Hastings and also by train from Hastings, Tunbridge Wells and London.

Refreshments
The New Eight Bells, the George Inn or the Seven Stars Inn. Or perhaps a picnic along the route.

Gray Nicholls — home of the cricket bat

Battle

Outline
Battle — Farthing Pond — Millers Farm — Battle.

Summary
Starting from the lane beside Battle Abbey Gatehouse this walk runs dowhill past Saxon Wood, offering a lovely view of Powdermill Wood at the bottom of the hill. Moving on into Powdermill Wood the route then skirts Farthing Pond before continuing beneath the trees to reach Powdermill Lane. A relaxing stroll along a long driveway to Millers Farm comes next with more far-reaching views along the way. Swinging back towards Battle the route then passes the charming Stone Cottage before once again crossing over Powdermill Lane and then for a short distance running alongside it. A fairly long slope then leads back towards Battle, with the remains of St Martin's Abbey visible from one point through the trees on the hillside over to the right. Once back in Battle a wide choice of refreshments is available from one of the many hospitable tearooms or pubs, perhaps before a visit to the abbey itself or the Battle Museum of Local History, Buckleys Yesterday's World, The Cricket Museum or The Almonry and Town Model. Keen shoppers will also be glad to know that Battle specialises in a wide range of small independent retail shops.

Attractions
By order of William the Conqueror the high altar of Battle Abbey, which was built in 1067 to celebrate his victory over the Saxons and was dedicted to St Martin, was placed on the spot where King Harold fell, the town of Battle subsequently developing around it. The start of this walk is near the huge Battle Abbey Gatehouse which was added in 1338 on the instruction of Abbot de Ketling. To be strictly accurate the Battle of Hastings is incorrectly named, its real location and therefore its real name being the Battle of Senlac Hill. Not that anyone is likely to want to 'do battle' over the matter, especially as they actually stand there themselves, perhaps with imaginations running riot as they try to picture that famous day-long struggle in 1066 when the Saxons, who had occupied Senlac Hill, were defeated by the Normans. The Bayeux Tapestry provides an account of that battle and visitors to Battle Abbey are offered an audio-visual presentation relating the story.

Stewards at the nearby 12th century St Mary's Church are on duty to welcome visitors and can give information about arranging special guided tours. Points of interest include a Romanesque nave and a Norman font with a medieval cover as well as rare 14th century wall paintings and also the tomb of Sir Anthony Browne, Master of the King's Horse, to whom Henry VIII granted the abbey after its dissolution in 1538.

Continued on page 64

Route 14

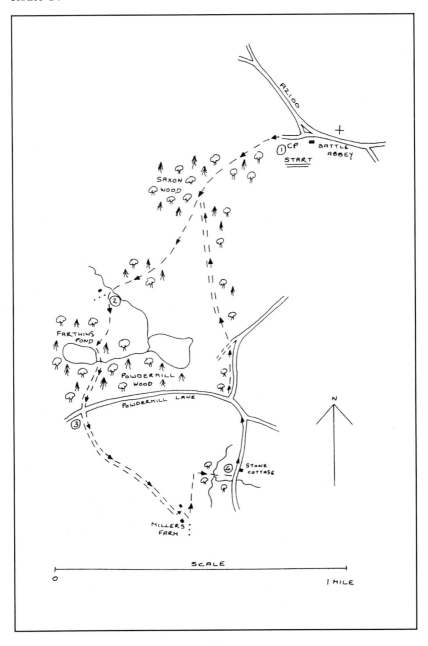

SCALE

0   1 MILE

Route 14

Battle

3½ miles

Start

At the Battle Abbey Ruins car park beside Battle Abbey in Park Lane (OS Pathfinder 1290 GR 748157), approached from High Street, which is an extension of London Road (A2100).

Route

1. *Turn left out of car park entrance into Park Lane. Proceed to end of lane and pass through a gateway. Bearing slightly left follow path leading downhill beside a fence (as indicated by yellow arrow). Cross over a stile beside a gate and continue along path still running beside fence. On reaching a fork proceed along indicated bridleway to the right. Cross over a stile beside a gate and continue straight ahead along bridleway leading through trees, eventually crossing over a small bridge.*

2. *Just beyond bridge cross over a stile on the left and, bearing slightly towards the right, cross through a field in direction indicated by yellow arrow. Cross over a stile and proceed along winding path through woods. Continue along the left side of a pond and cross over a small footbridge (CAUTION). Continue as path leads into a track, proceeding uphill in direction of yellow arrow. Continue along track to reach a lane.*

3. *Cross over lane (Powdermill Lane) (CAUTION) and proceed along Millers Farm driveway as indicated by stone footpath sign. On eventually reaching Millers Farm cross over indicated stile on the left. Bearing slightly right proceed downhill beside fence and after about 50 yards/metres turn left and cross through field in direction of footpath sign. Cross over a stile and turn right, proceeding downhill along border of a field (as indicated by footpath sign). Cross over a footbridge and then over a stile and proceed along right border of another field as indicated by yellow arrow.*

4. *Cross over a stile and turn left at a lane (CAUTION). Proceed along lane and on reaching a T-junction turn left into another lane. Proceed along this lane to reach Powdermill Lane. Cross over Powdermill Lane and follow indicated footpath leading uphill beneath trees. Continue along path as it runs uphill along right border of a field. Cross over a dirt track at the top of the hill and then cross over a stile, proceeding straight ahead through a field in direction of footpath sign. Cross over a stile beside a gate and follow track downhill through a field. Cross over another stile beside a gate and continue along track which then leads along right border of another field. Cross over yet another stile beside another gate and continue along track which then leads uphill along right border of another field. Continue over brow of hill to rejoin earlier section of walk. Continue straight ahead, retracing steps to car park.*

Powdermill Lane is named after the gunpowder mill which between 1676 and 1874 reputedly produced over a ton of gunpowder every day. A torchlight procession and the Normus Gurt Bonfire and fireworks display is held here every year in November, where the Battle Guy, which in 1686 was the first guy in Britain, traditionally 'meets his maker'. In fact throughout the year there is an appealing diary of special events in Battle, including an annual Marbles Match and Easter Bonnet Parade on Good Friday, the Battle Festival and Medieval Fair in May, Battle in Bloom between June and September and Gala Late Night Shopping in December. There are also weekly markets, antique sales and wine-tastings in local vineyards, further details of which are available from the local Tourist Information Centres.

Such a fascinating range of attractions together with the spectacular beauty of the surrounding countryside make this an ideal family outing and one that may well, by popular demand, be repeated, the natural calendar of events in the fields and woods throughout the seasons offering as much variety as events in the town.

Access by bus and train
To Battle by bus from Hastings and Bexhill and also by train from Hastings, Tunbridge Wells and London.

Refreshments
At the Pilgrims Rest Tearoom beside the gatehouse, which used to be a hostel for pilgrims on their way to Canterbury, or at one of the many other delightful tearooms or pubs in the town.

Approach to Battle Abbey gatehouse

Northiam

Outline
Northiam − Great Dixter − Strawberry Hole Cottage − Northiam.

Summary
Starting in front of the church, with its impressive 16th century stone spire, this route leads first through part of the peaceful, pretty village of Northiam before passing the 15th century former manor house of Great Dixter, a fine timber-framed, crooked building which is well-known for its lovely garden, a flame of colour in May when pink-tinged white rhododendrons blossom abundantly beside a tranquil pond. Panoramic views over the lovely surrounding countryside open out in all directions on the gentle descent that follows, before the route joins a beautiful section of the Sussex Border Path, where in May shady havens beside a relaxing tinkling stream are lit up with wildflowers, such as bluebells and white-petalled ramsons and where children can enjoy crossing over neat little wooden footbridges and a series of sometimes rather challenging stiles. An easy climb through more rich farmland near Strawberry Hole Cottage then leads back to Northiam.

Attractions
A visit to almost any village in East Sussex has its own undeniable charm, providing an ideal outlet, particularly for those whose lives are more usually and often rather suffocatingly city-bound. Yet it is out there in the surrounding hills, valleys, fields and woods where the real pulse of country life can be felt, a world full of memorable natural sights and sounds, where the regular motion of the constantly changing seasons offers endless variety and occasional wonderful surprises. Even the best descriptions sometimes fail to measure up to the pleasure of first-hand experience, the unforgettable delight for example of suddenly spotting a sheep deftly shooing away an over-audacious pheasant, which is forced to run for cover under a nearby bush or hedge, or perhaps the sight of a tiny white lamb with huge fluffy balls of wool around its ankles like a pair of luxury socks, its little tail wagging frantically as it dives somewhat violently under its mother for a vigorous drink of her milk. Bird-watchers, whether experts or beginners, might see skylarks hovering on high, robins perched perhaps on a post as if on guard, magpies spreading their wide, colourful wings as they take off in search of food for their young and orange-beaked blackbirds, possibly amongst the best whistlers of the wild. Few, however, will ever see the cuckoo, although its call can often be heard in spring, sounding just like its name, coming from the depths of a peaceful wood. Wildflowers in both spring and summer generously pepper the landscape, including the deep pink herb Robert, the white lesser celandine, the yellow archangel with its reddish markings on the inside of its petals and the small, but striking early purple orchid, with its distinctive black-spotted leaves.

Continued on page 68

Route 15

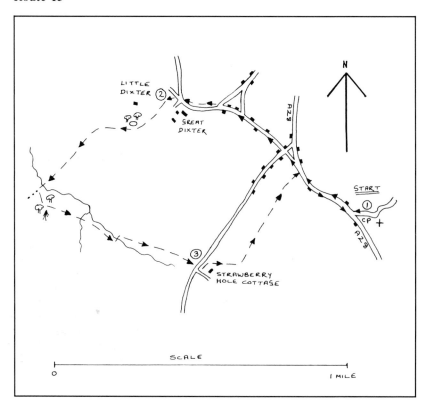

Route 15

Northiam
3 miles

Start
At Northiam car park in Main Street (OS Pathfinder Sheet TQ 82/92 GR 829245), which is part of the A28.

Route

1. *Turn left out of car park entrance and then immediately right into Main Street. Continue along Main Street and, just past the Crown and Thistle, turn left into Dixter Road. Continue along Dixter Road and on reaching a fork take left turn in direction of signpost to Great Dixter. On reaching the signposted entrance to Great Dixter follow indicated Ewhurst footpath to the right of the driveway. Continue as path leads into driveway. After a further 20 yards/metres bear slightly left and cross over a cattle grid.*

2. *Turn left along indicated Ewhurst footpath, which leads downhill along irregular left border of a field. Cross a stile in far left corner and then, bearing slightly right, cross downhill through another field in direction of a yellow arrow. Cross over a stile and continue downhill through another field in direction of another yellow arrow. Cross over a footbridge and turn left to join the Sussex Border Path. Continue through a small band of woods and then proceed through a field in direction of yellow arrow. Cross over another footbridge and continue along left border of another field. After several hundred yards/metres turn left in direction of yellow arrow and cross over a small bridge closely followed by a stile. Turn right and follow right border of a field, eventually crossing over a stile beside a gate.*

3. *Cross over a lane (CAUTION) and enter the driveway of Strawberry Hole, turning left almost immediately along indicated Sussex Border Path beside Strawbery Hole Cottage. After several hundred yards/metres cross over a stile and, bearing slightly towards the right, proceed uphill through another field. Cross over a stile and, bearing slightly left, follow indicated path uphill through another field towards Northiam. Pass through a gap in a hedge and continue straight ahead along the left border of two playing fields to reach Main Street. Turn right (CAUTION) and retrace steps to car park.*

Access by bus and steam train
To Northiam by bus from Rye and by steam train from Tenterden.

A children's playground near the end of the walk might be just the answer for youngsters with any surplus energy and the whole family might then enjoy a journey on the Kent and East Sussex Railway from Northiam Station to Tenterden, or a boat trip along the River Rother to Bodiam Castle, leaving from the moorings just beyond the railway's level crossing. (Routes through the countryside around Tenterden and Bodiam Castle are described in *Family Walks in the Weald of Kent and Sussex*).

Refreshments
At the Crown and Thistle public house.

Footbridge near Great Dixter

Rye Harbour

Outline

Rye Harbour – Rye Harbour Nature Reserve – River Rother Estuary – Rye Harbour.

Summary

Lovers of nature can be sure of a visual feast on this short, undemanding walk through the Rye Harbour Nature Reserve, a flat, remote and starkly beautiful corner of the East Sussex coastline. Not that any particular degree of expertise on the subject is required either. A wealth of information can be found at the small information centre in the car park and in addition comprehensive colour charts of birds are displayed on the wooden walls of two ideal public hides where the often difficult business of identification becomes almost literally mere child's play. The shingled beach is a good spot for a picnic, a place where brown hares might be seen and also, in late May and June, a colourful array of wildflowers. Finally, as the route runs alongside the River Rother, the atmosphere is completed with the pretty picture of yachts and motor launches easing their way between the estuary and Rye Harbour.

Attractions

The walk begins beside a Martello Tower, one of several built along the coast to defend Britain from the French during the Napoleonic War. Once through the adjacent holiday caravan park the footpath is flanked on both sides by open farmland before entering the Rye Harbour Nature Reserve. Designated by the Nature Conservancy Council as a Site of Special Scientific Interest, the area is a large tract of shingle ridges which were formed as the sea receded over a period of hundreds of years. Home to beach-nesting seabirds for centuries, it is now regarded as having one of the finest examples of coastal shingle vegetation in England, with over 300 species of flowering plants. Perhaps not so immediately appealing, yet vital in the natural cycle, it also has a reputation as the most important site for invertebrates in East Sussex, with over 1,500 species of moths, beetles, flies and spiders so far recorded. Happy about that is the Marsh Frog which can be heard croaking loudly throughout the summer.

As indicated on a large map at the car park information centre this walk can be lengthened by turning right at the seafront and then doubling back further along the beach. Time should be left, though, for at least a short stroll around the famous town of Rye, which as well as the nearby Winchelsea was one of two 'Antient Townes' belonging to the Confederation of Cinque Ports. In return for special privileges in trade and fishing the confederation was obliged to provide ships for the Royal Navy during the Hundred Years War with France. Along with many other Sussex towns Rye was attacked repeatedly between 1337 and 1448 and was extensively damaged. So too were the forests of the Weald, with oak trees being felled not only to build

Continued on page 72

Route 16

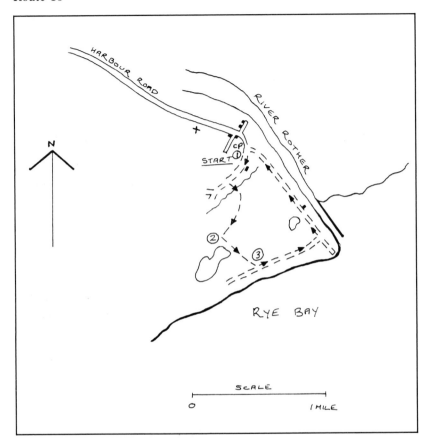

Route 16

Rye Harbour $2\frac{1}{2}$ miles

Start

At the public car park in Rye Harbour, which is at the end of Harbour Road, about two miles south of Rye (OS Landranger 189 GR 942190). The way to Rye Harbour is indicated by regular signposts from central Rye.

Route

1. *Turn right out of main car park entrance and follow the signposted footpath which leads along the driveway into Frenchman's Beach Holiday Village. About a hundred yards/metres past the Frenchman's Beach Club turn left along a raised grassy pathway, which leads across a high concrete footbridge (CAUTION). Continue along raised pathway.*

2. *Follow path as it swings sharply left and after about a further hundred yards/ metres pass through a kissing gate into signposted Rye Harbour Nature Reserve. Continue along pathway, eventually reaching a tarmac track which runs along the top of the shingled beach.*

3. *Turn left into tarmac track. On reaching the estuary of the River Rother turn left again and follow tarmac path all the way back to Rye Harbour and the car park.*

Access by bus

To Rye Harbour from Rye, which is reached by bus from most nearby towns.

Redshank

71

more ships but also to fuel the iron industry required for weaponry. On the drive back from Rye Harbour, with the impressive sight of Rye ahead, perched on top of a sandstone hill, it is interesting and almost easy to imagine those early days, when the town was battered by a natural adversary too, the sea, which by the end of the 15th century had finally ebbed away, leaving the former port well and truly inland.

Refreshments
At the William The Conqueror public house or perhaps a picnic on the shingled beach.

Rye Harbour

Useful information

Walks in order of difficulty

Starting with the easiest

Route 16 — Rye Harbour (2½ miles)
Route 14 — Battle (3½ miles)
Route 4 — Uckfield and Buxted Deer Park (4½ miles)
Route 1 — Harrison's Rocks (2½ miles)
Route 6 — Upper Dicker (3½ miles)
Route 5 — Barcombe (4 miles)
Route 12 — Ticehurst and Bewl Water (4 miles)
Route 11 — Wood's Corner (3½ miles)
Route 7 — Alfriston (2½ miles)
Route 8 — Birling Gap (Seven Sisters Cliff) (3½ miles)
Route 15 — Northiam (3 miles)
Route 9 — Windmill Hill and Herstmonceux Castle (3½ miles)
Route 3 — Duddleswell (Ashdown Forest) (3½ miles)
Route 13 — Robertsbridge (4 miles)
Route 2 — Hartfield (4 miles)
Route 10 — Punnett's Town (3 miles)

Public transport in East Sussex

The area covered by this book is fairly well serviced by public transport although careful study of timetables is essential since some services tend to be infrequent.

For details of operators and timetables contact the following:

Autopoint (Hailsham). Tel. 0323 832430.
Bexhill Bus Company. Tel. 0424 211563.
Brighton and Hove Bus and Coach Co. Tel. 0273 206666.
Brighton Buses. Tel. 0273 674881.
British Rail (Brighton). Tel. 0273 206755.
Eastbourne Buses. Tel. 0323 416416.
East Sussex Rider Services. Tel. 0273 478007.
East Sussex County Council (Highways and Transportation). Tel. 0273 482123.
Hastings Buses. Tel. 0424 433711.
Haven Coaches. Tel. 0273 517417.
J&H Coaches (Bexhill-on-Sea). Tel. 0424 731839.
Lewes Coaches. Tel. 0273 674881.
Rambler Coaches (St Leonards-on-Sea). Tel. 0424 752505.
RDH Services (Lewes). Tel. 0273 400711.
Rye Coaches. Tel. 0797 226949.
South Coast Buses. Tel. 0424 433711.
Southdown Bus Station (Lewes). Tel. 0273 474441.
    or (Eastbourne). Tel. 0323 27354.
Sussex Bus (Bognor Regis). Tel. 0243 264492.
Warrens Coaches Ltd (Ticehurst). Tel. 0580 200226.
Wealden — Beeline (Tunbridge Wells). Tel. 0892 833830.
Whites Coaches (Heathfield). Tel. 0435 863485.

Tourist Information Centres

Battle, 88 High Street. Tel. 0424 773721.
Bexhill-on-Sea, De La Warr Pavilion, Marina. Tel. 0424 212023.

Boship, Boship Roundabout, Lower Dicker. Tel. 0323 442667.
Brighton, 10 Bartholomew Square. Tel. 0273 323755.
Eastbourne, Cornfield Road. Tel. 0323 411400.
Hailsham, The Library, Western Road. Tel. 0323 840604.
Hastings, 4 Robertson Terrace. Tel. 0424 718888.
Hove, Norton Road. Tel. 0273 778087.
Hove, King Alfred Leisure Centre, Kingsway. Tel. 0273 746100.
Lewes, Lewes House, High Street. Tel. 0273 483448.
Peacehaven, Meridian Centre, Roderick Avenue. Tel. 0273 582668.
Pevensey, Pevensey Castle, High Street. Tel. 0323 761444.
Rye, Heritage Centre, Strand Quay. Tel. 0797 226696.
Seaford, Station Approach. Tel. 0323 897426.

Pond near Upper Dicker (route 6)

74

Wet weather alternatives in East Sussex

Completely or partly under cover. It is advisable to check times of opening before a visit, is made.

Museums and craft workshops

Alfriston Heritage Centre and Blacksmiths' Museum. Tel. 0323 870303 Museum and Pony House. Local history display. Shop. Open April to October.

Anne of Cleves House Museum, Lewes. Tel. 0273 474610. Sussex history display and Tudor garden. Shop. Open April to October.

Bexhill Museum. Tel. 0424 211769. Local history, shop and picnic site. Open February to December.

Booth Museum of Natural History, Brighton. Tel. 0273 552586. Bird and butterfly display, natural history. Shop. Open all year.

Brighton Museum and Art Gallery. Tel. 0273 603005. Art and costume display. Shop and tearoom. Open all year.

British Engineerium, Hove. Tel. 0273 559583. Museum of living steam. Models, tools and restored engines. Shop and refreshments. Open all year.

Buckleys Yesterday's World, Battle. Tel. 04246 4269. Vivid scenes of life from Edwardian times to middle of this century. Recreated period shops, penny arcade, 1930's railway station, and small garden. Shop and refreshments. Open all year.

Ditchling Museum. Tel. 0273 844744. Local history exhibition in former Victorian school. Shop and refreshments. Open all year.

Filching Manor Motor Museum, Polegate. Tel. 0323 487838. Impressive collection of cars including Sir Malcolm Campbell's 1937 Bluebird. Additional art and antique displays. Shop, refreshments and picnic site. Open Easter to October.

Foredown Tower Countryside Centre, Hove. Tel. 0273 422540. Local history exhibition in 1900's converted water tower. Shop and picnic site. Open all year.

Hastings Museum and Art Gallery. Tel. 0424 721202. Natural history, art, pottery, ironwork and ceramic displays. Shop. Open all year.

Heaven Farm Country Tours and Museum, Furners Green, near Uckfield. Tel. 0825 790226. Display of agricultural equipment and tools, nature trail and farm animals. Shop, tearoom and picnic site. Open March to November.

Hove Museum and Art Gallery. Tel. 0273 779410. Art and local history. Tearoom. Open all year.

How We Lived Then Museum of Shops and Social History, Eastbourne. Tel. 0323 37143. Exhibition portraying life between 1850 and 1950. Shop. Open February to December.

Lewes Living History Model. Tel. 0273 486290. Audio-visual introduction to Lewes, illustrating history from Saxon times. Shop and refreshments. Open all year.

Newhaven Fort. Tel. 0273 517622. Victorian fort built in the 1860's. Military museum and children's play area. Shop, refreshments and picnic site. Open April to October.

Pooks Hill Toy Museum, Burwash Weald. Tel. 0435 882072. Private collection of toys from turn of the century to present day displayed in old Victorian shop. Open April to September.

Quarry Farm Rural Experience, Bodiam. Tel. 0580 830670. Exhibition of privately-owned steam engines. Open April to September.

Ripley's Museum of Rural Life, Robertsbridge. Tel. 0580 880324. Working forge in blacksmith and wheelwright's shop. Agricultural display. Shop and picnic site. Open all year.

Rye Museum, Ypres Tower. Tel. 0797 226728. Local history display in 13th century tower and former jail. Open April to October.

Seaford Museum of Local History. Tel. 0323 898222. Maritime displays. Shop. Open all year.

Shipwreck Heritage Centre, Hastings. Tel. 0424 437452. Sound and light show depicting medieval shipwreck. Also maritime display. Shop. Open April to September.

Sussex Farm Museum, Horam, near Heathfield. Tel. 04353 2597. Farm museum, nature trail, craft and old farming method demonstrations. Restaurant and picnic site. Open Easter to October.

Sussex Toy and Model Museum, Brighton. Tel. 0273 749494. Collection of toys and models displayed in the arches beneath the railway station. Shop and refreshments. Open all year.
The Cricket Museum, Battle. Details from Tourist Information Centre, tel. 0424 773721. A display showing cricket through the ages.
Thomas Smith (Herstmonceux). Tel. 0323 832137. Traditional Sussex trug basket making on view. Shop. Open all year.
Towner Art Gallery and Local History Museum, Eastbourne. Tel. 0323 411688. Art and local history displays in 18th century house. Shop. Open all year.

Castles and houses

Alfriston Clergy House. Tel. 0323 870001. 14th century thatched and half-timbered house. The first to be acquired by the National Trust in 1896. Open April to October.
Bateman's, Burwash. Tel. 0435 882302. Rudyard Kipling's home between 1902 and 1936. Display of his rooms and study; working water mill and gardens. Open April to October.
Battle Abbey. Tel. 04246 3792. The Battle of Hastings was fought here in 1066. The abbey was founded by William the Conqueror. Open all year.
Bentley Estate, near Lewes. Tel. 0825 840573. Tudor farmhouse with collection of furniture and paintings. Also collection of vintage cars, gardens, tearoom, picnic and play area with miniature steam railway. Open daily March to October.
Bodiam Castle, near Robertsbridge. Tel. 0580 830436. 14th century castle erected to block the Rother Valley as a defence against a feared invasion by the French. Excellent views from some of the towers. Open April to October.
Boughton Monchelsea Place, Boughton Monchelsea. Tel. 0622 743120. Elizabethan manor house built of Kentish ragstone in 1567. Exhibitions of items from clothes to farm implements. Views over deer park. Open Easter to October. Refreshments.
Brickwall House and Gardens, Northiam. Tel. 0797 223329. Beautiful gardens with 18th century bowling alley, sunken topiary garden and chess garden. Open April to September.
Charleston Farmhouse, near Lewes. Tel. 0323 811265. 17th-18th century farmhouse, former home of artists Vanessa and Clive Bell and Duncan Grant, member of 'The Bloomsbury Set'. Garden, shop and exhibition. Open April to October.
Firle Place, near Lewes. Tel. 0273 858335. Collection of part of the Cowper Collection of paintings. Shop, restaurant and picnic site. Open April to September.
Glynde Place, near Lewes. Tel. 0273 858337. 16th century home of Viscount Hampden. Exhibition of historic portraits and bronzes. Coach house cafe. Open April to September.
Great Dixter House and Gardens, Northiam. Tel. 0797 253160. 15th century manor house with great hall restored by Sir Edward Lutyens, who also designed the attractive gardens. Refreshments. Open April to October.
Hammerwood Park, near Forest Row. Tel. 0342 850594. Lovingly restored building with displays of furniture, costumes and agricultural implements. Refreshments. Open April to September.
Haremere Hall, Etchingham. Tel. 058081 245. Tudor manor house with terraced gardens including nature trail and picnic site. Refreshments. Ring for details of opening.
Hastings Castle and 1066 Story. Tel. 0424 717963. Remains of Norman castle built after William the Conqueror's victory at the Battle of Hastings. 1066 Story Interpretation Centre. Picnic site. Open all year.
Lamb House, Rye. Tel. 0797 223763. Georgian home of author Henry James between 1898 and 1916. Display of furniture, pictures and personal memorabilia. Open April to October.
Lewes Castle. Tel. 0273 486290. Norman castle with good views. Restored 14th century gateway. Open all year.
Michelham Priory, Upper Dicker. Tel. 0323 844224. 13th century moated priory with 14th century gatehouse. Wide variety of displays, craft and rope museum, working watermill, shop, restaurant and picnic site. Open March to November.

Monks House, Rodmell, near Lewes. Tel. 0892 890651. Converted farmhouse, former home of Virginia Woolf. Display of furniture and personal memorabilia. Restored garden with ponds and walkways. Open April to October.

Pevensey Castle. Tel. 0323 762604. Remains of Roman Saxon shore fort. Special events. Tearoom. Open all year.

Preston Manor. Tel. 0273 603005. Georgian manor owned for two centuries by the Stanford family. Collection of furniture, personal possessions and art. Open all year.

Royal Pavilion, Brighton. Tel. 0273 603005. Enormous and unforgettably striking Eastern-style palace of Prince Regent, later George IV. Restored Music Room and Queen Victoria's apartments on display. Shop and tearoom. Open all year.

Sheffield Park Garden, near Uckfield. Tel. 0825 790655. Garden designed in 18th century with five split-level lakes and display of rare trees and shrubs. Open April to November.

Trains, farms, vineyards and wildlife attractions

A Smuggler's Adventure at St Clement's Caves, Hastings. Tel. 0424 422964. The story of 18th and 19th century smuggling along the Kent and Sussex coasts, enhanced with sound and lighting effects. Shop. Open all year.

Ashdown Forest Farm, Wych Cross. Tel. 082571 2040. Survival Centre approved by the Rare Breeds Survival Trust for endangered species not usually found on modern farms. Special calendar of events from lambing and ploughing to rural crafts and sheep-shearing. Refreshments at farm shop or picnic with view over Ashdown Forest. Open daily except Christmas.

Barkham Manor Vineyard, Piltdown, near Uckfield. Tel. 082572 2103. Walks, winery, museum, farm animals. Restaurant and tearoom. Open all year.

Barnsgate Manor Vineyards, Uckfield. Tel. 082571 3366. Ring for details of tours, meals and winetasting.

Bartley Mill, Bell's Yew Green. Tel. 0892 890372. Formerly a hop farm, now milling organic wheat. Craft shop, museum and farm trail. Open all year except Christmas period. Refreshments and picnic site.

Horse grazing in field behind Lullington Farm House (route 7)

77

Battle Town Model Show and Almonry Gardens. Tel. 04246 2727. Scale model of Battle with narration, sound effects and lighting. Shop and restaurant. Open all year.

Bentley Wildfowl and Motor Museum, Bentley, near Lewes. Tel. 0825 840573. Great Britain's largest collection of rare wildfowl. Also collection of vintage cars. Miniature steam railway on summer Sundays.

Bluebell Railway, Uckfield. Tel. 082572 2370. Steam railway rides between Sheffield Park and Horsted Keynes. Open all year except Christmas and Boxing Day.

Brighton Marina Village. Tel. 0273 693636. Britain's largest yacht marina. Shops, bars and cinema. Open all year.

Brighton Sea Life Centre. Tel. 0273 604234. Displays of marine life including a whale and dolphin exhibition. Shop and refreshments. Open all year.

Carr Taylor Vineyards, Hastings. Tel. 0424 752501. Vineyard trail, winetasting. Shop and picnic site. Open all year.

Children's World, Great Knelle, Beckley, near Rye. Tel. 0797 260250. Conducted tractor train tour of rare animal breed farm, adventure playground, fishing, craft shops, picnic area and refreshments bar. Open March to September.

Drusillas Park, Alfriston. Tel. 0323 870234. Zoo, adventure playground, rail tour through animal paddocks, a variety of craft, gift and toy shops, with refreshment facilities including playland food bar, pub, snackbar and restaurant. Open all year.

Five Chimneys Vineyards, Uckfield. Tel. 082581 3159. Ring for details of tours, meals and winetasting.

Flimwell Bird Park, Flimwell. Tel. 0580 87202. Exotic waterfowl, swans, pheasants, 14 acres of woodland, children's playground, picnic area and refreshments bar. Open April to October.

Fort Fun, Eastbourne. Tel. 0323 642833. Children's adventure playground, indoor soft play centre (The Apache Trail) and fun park with runaway train rides and roller coaster. Refreshments and picnic site. Open all year.

Hastings Sea Life Centre. Tel. 0424 718776. Marine life display including octopus and sharks. Shop and restaurant. Open all year.

Heaven Farm, Uckfield. Tel. 0825 790177. Nature trail and museum with guided tours. Open all year. Refreshments.

Lavender Line Steam Museum, Isfield, near Uckfield. Tel. 082575 515. Rides on vintage steam train with museum and buffet coach. Open March to December.

Leeford Vineyards, Whatlington, near Battle. Tel. 04246 3183. Vineyard, oasthouse shop and picnic site. Open April to December.

Merriments Gardens, Hurst Green. Tel. 0580 860666. Four-acre garden including water gardens and orchard. Shop and tearoom. Open March to October.

Merrydown Wine, near Heathfield. Tel. 04353 2254. Tours through cider and winemaking factory. Open Tuesday to Friday, Easter to October.

Planet Earth at Garden Paradise, Newhaven. Tel. 0273 512123. Gardens, adventure playground and Planet Earth displays, including motorised dinosaurs and earthquakes. Shop, restaurant and picnic site. Open all year.

Rye Town Model Sound and Light Show. Tel. 0797 226696. Half-hour presentation of the history of Rye, with sound and light effects. Shop. Open all year.

St George's Vineyard, Waldron, near Heathfield. Tel. 04353 2156. Vineyard and shop. Also restaurant. Open March to December.

Seven Sisters Sheep Centre, East Dean, near Eastbourne. Tel. 0323 423302. Working sheep farm with seasonal demonstrations, a shop with dairy products and a pets corner. Open March to September.

Southover Grange Gardens, Lewes. Tel. 0273 472555. 16th century house and gardens, once home to diarist John Evelyn. Refreshments. Open all year.

Stoneywish Country Park, Ditchling. Tel. 0273 843498. Ponds and lakeside walks, farm animals, children's play area and local history display. Tearoom and picnic site. Open all year.

The Living World, Seaford. Tel. 0323 870100. Natural history display in restored Sussex barn. Walks, shop and refreshments. Open all year.

The Sussex Shire Horses, Etchingham. Tel. 058081 501. Home of 30 horses including Shires, Suffolk Punches, Ardennes, Cart Horses and Heavy Work Cobs. Demonstrations and presentations with a view to promoting conservation and care for the environment. Open daily July to September.

Treasure Island, Eastbourne. Tel. 0323 411077. Children's adventure playground. Refreshments and picnic site. Open April to October.

West Blatchington Windmill, Hove. Tel. 0273 775400. Hexagonal 19th century smock mill with remounted sweeps. Museum. Open May to September.

Wilderness Wood, Hadlow Down, near Uckfield. Tel. 0825 830509. Woodland trail, wood management displays and children's play areas. Shop, refreshments and barbecue site. Open all year.

Sporting facilities

Claverham Community College Sports Centre, Battle. Tel. 0424 772302.
Dolphin Leisure Centre, Haywards Heath. Tel. 0444 457337.
Downs Leisure Centre, Seaford. Tel. 0323 490011.
King Alfred Leisure Centre, Brighton. Tel. 0273 822228.
Lewes Leisure Centre, Lewes. Tel. 0273 486000.
Portslade Sports Centre, Brighton. Tel. 0273 411100.
Utopia, Uckfield's Leisure Centre, Uckfield. Tel. 0825 761722.

Bibliography

Jim Cleland, *The Visitor's Guide to Sussex*, 1990.
Miles Jebb, *A Guide to the Southdowns Way*, 1984.
Roger Penn, *Portrait of Ashdown Forest*, 1984.
Warden Swinfen & David Arscott, *Hidden Sussex*, 1984.
Edited by John Hadfield, *The Shell Book of English Villages*, 1980.
Michael H.C. Baker, *Sussex Villages*, 1977.
Roy Milward & Adrian Robinson, *South East England: The Channel Coastlands*, 1973.

Old Clergy House (route 7)

THE FAMILY WALKS SERIES

The publishers welcome suggestions for further titles in this series; and will be pleased to consider manuscripts relating to Derbyshire from new or established authors.

Scarthin Books of Cromford, in the Peak District, are also leading second-hand and antiquarian booksellers, and are eager to purchase specialised material, both ancient and modern.

Contact Dr D.J. Mitchell, 0629-823272.